I0139466

Living on the South Side of the Tracks:
The River Street Digital History Project and Boise, Idaho

William A. White, III

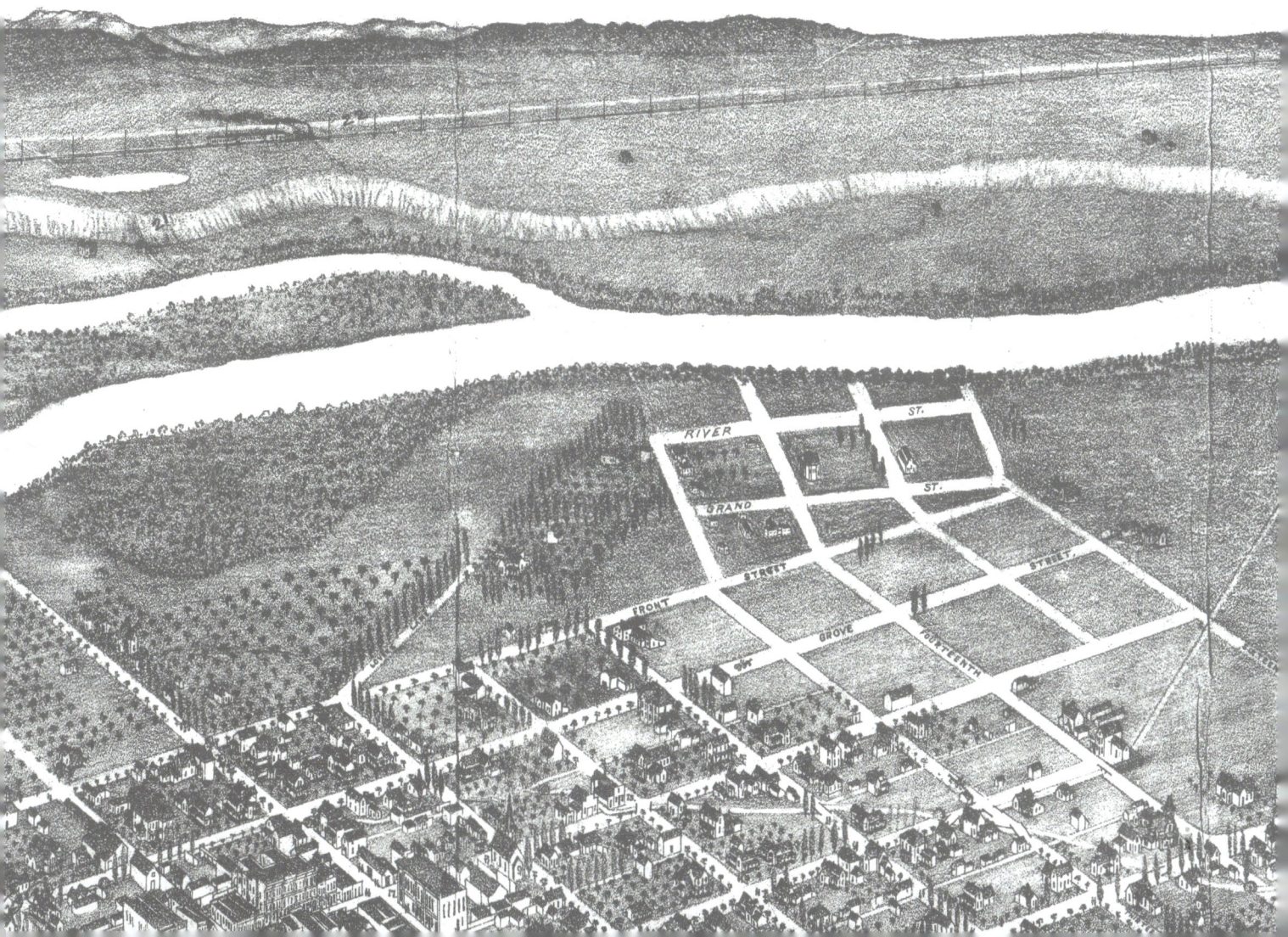

Living on the South Side of the Tracks:
The River Street Digital History Project and Boise, Idaho

BY

William A. White, III

Copyediting and Book Design by Nicole C. Lavely

Boise City Department of Arts and History | Charles Redd Center for Western Studies | The University of Arizona

Oral histories are narrative texts and interpretations of past events created from the memories of those who lived them. Newspaper articles are another form of narrative text conveyed by informants who were also using their memory to describe interpretations of lived events. This document has been prepared in good faith on the basis of information available at the date of publication as best recalled by former residents of the River Street Neighborhood and available archival materials. The author will not be liable for any loss, damage, cost or expense incurred or arising by reason of any person using or relying on information in this publication.

ISBN 978-0692701898

This work is licensed under the Creative Commons Attribution Non-Commercial ShareAlike 4.0 International License. To view a copy of this license, visit:
http://creativecommons.org/licenses/by-nc-sa/4.0/

Acknowledgements

Good, generous people are behind every digital history project. There is a large cast of characters that directly contributed to this project's success.

Before there was a digital history project, there was an idea. I was fortunate enough to be helped in my initial investigations by my good friend Pam Demo. Much of my work builds upon the firm foundation established by her MA Thesis, *Boise's River Street Neighborhood: Lee, Ash, and Lover's Lane/Pioneer Streets: The South Side of the Tracks*. Early on, I was also able to gain the support of Dr. Jill Gill of Boise State University who, coincidentally, is working on a project that parallels this research in River Street. She has been an excellent and generous collaborator.

I owe a special thanks to the "South Side of the Tracks Kids" who allowed me to attend their 2013 reunion and put up with my pesky questions. I also owe a heartfelt thanks to the members of St. Paul Baptist Church of Boise who have generously offered to let me delve into their memories for this project.

A host of other folks selflessly helped me collect, digitize, and process the archival materials for this project. I would like to sincerely thank Michal Davidson and the rest of the staff at the Idaho State Historical Society Archives in Boise; along with Belinda Davis, Mary Anne Davis, and Shannon Vihlene at the Idaho State Historic Preservation Office for their time and effort. The staff at the Albertsons Library at Boise State University and the Boise Public Library provided invaluable support locating and digitizing documents related to urban renewal and the River Street Neighborhood.

I would also like to thank Cannon Daughtrey and Rita Sulkosky for their remarkable GIS and map digitization work. You guys really brought those maps to life.

Most importantly, I would like to thank those that gave me the first interviews for this book: John Bertram, Dick Madry, Lee Rice, II, and Warner Terrell, III. Without your time and generosity, this project would not have been possible.

Funding

In addition to time and effort, financial support for the 2014 field-work was provided by the following groups:

The Boise City Department of Arts and History who provided a Boise Arts and History grant that was used for the development of this book;

The Charles Redd Center for Western Studies who provided travel funding; and

The University of Arizona where I received invaluable advice on how to conceive and execute this project and provided project funding for other aspects of this research.

Thanks to all who helped make this project a success. I apologize if I have forgotten to mention you by name, but I assure you, I truly appreciate your help.

Sincerely,

Bill White
PhD Student
School of Anthropology
University of Arizona

Figure 1. (Title Page Image) Bird's eye view of Boise, c.1887 (courtesy of the Idaho State Archives).

Table of Contents

List of Figures

Introduction

Race relations remain a central issue in American politics, economics, and culture. Interactions between African Americans and Euroamericans have been a focal point of historical archaeology for the last 30 years. The River Street Digital History Project is centered on the River Street Neighborhood, which was the historical home for most of the non-white population of Boise. The content of this book is the fruits of the research that was collected as part of this digital research project, which was conducted in the summer of 2014 in anticipation of historical archaeological excavations in the River Street Neighborhood.

The neighborhood has long been known as the historical home for Boise's African American population, however a diverse population of Euroamericans, Japanese workers, Basque, and other European immigrants also called this place home. While River Street was part of Boise's society and history, until the 1960s it was largely defined by the way it was segregated from the rest of town. The neighborhood was characterized by its diversity and color, which was considered undesirable by the majority of other Boiseans until after the Civil Rights Movement. The River Street Digital History Project attempts to capture the archival, oral history, and geographic information about this enclave and make it available to a much wider audience. It will also serve as the foundation for future archaeological investigations

The research in this book focuses on two principal questions:

What role did race play in the lives of River Street Neighborhood residents?

How did the racialization of African Americans by Euroamericans effect the creation of whiteness as a racial construct?

The River Street Digital History project centers on the creation of a website designed to disseminate digital copies of existing archival data, short segments of newly collected oral history interviews, and photographs from private collections. The website also supports a Google Earth-based Global Information System (GIS) file that can be used to take a self-guided or virtual tour of the River Street Neighborhood using a smartphone, tablet, or computer. The Google Earth tour is also linked to the reminiscences of former neighborhood residents. You can see historical photographs of a number of historical locations as they once were. Finally, a YouTube channel has been created for this project. Website visitors will be able to see short videos about the history of River Street and other aspects of the digital history project.

Most importantly, the website is an accretive vehicle that will grow as research continues.

Pictures, documents, and oral history summaries can be added as they are collected, which means the River Street Digital History Project will never be fully completed. There will always be more data that can and will be added. The result is a living compendium of historical data in an easily accessible format highlighting the interesting and unique history of Boise's largest multi-ethnic and multi-racial enclave.

In addition to providing a useful resource for Boiseans, historians interested in race relations in the United States, and others, this digital history project is also a vehicle for collecting information that will form the foundation of my doctoral project for my PhD in anthropology at the University of Arizona. The collected data will allow me to create an archaeological research design that addresses the questions that count for the local community and adds to what is known about racial interactions in Boise. The collected data will be put to work on a public archaeology project during the summer of 2015.

As is the story with other multi-ethnic enclaves, the River Street Neighborhood was born from the pervasive discrimination that existed throughout Idaho and the American West. Stories told by neighborhood residents, both black and white, reveal a place where people found a way to coexist with each other despite the garish racial and ethnic categories that dictated behavior within the surrounding community. It is this story of coexistence, cooperation, and perseverance that is at the heart of what it means to be a Boisean. Telling that story is the goal of this project. In the process, the digital history project will help fill a large gap in the history of race relations in Idaho.

Visit www.riverstreethistory.com for an introductory video of the River Street Digital History Project and more.

Figure 2. Bernease Rice and her son Lee, II in River Street, c.1950 (from the collection of Lee Rice II).

Data Collection and Distribution Strategies

A combination of traditional and modern data collection techniques were used to collect and disseminate information via the website. It was essential to use as many low-cost software platforms due to budget constraints and the desire to make this process possible for communities around the world. In addition to making the website accessible to a wide audience, it was important to be completely transparent with the software, methods, and concepts employed to make this project a reality. We wanted to be able to show others what and how the project was executed so that it can be replicated elsewhere. The result was an attractive website created through an easily replicable system that can be reproduced and improved upon by others.

Archival Research Methods

The River Street Neighborhood is a small portion of the City of Boise, which helped focus archival research on a specific geographic area. Most archival research focused on certain keywords; specifically, neighborhood landmarks, such as Riverside Park, street names, buildings, historical residents, and variations of the term "River Street Neighborhood". Online searches for

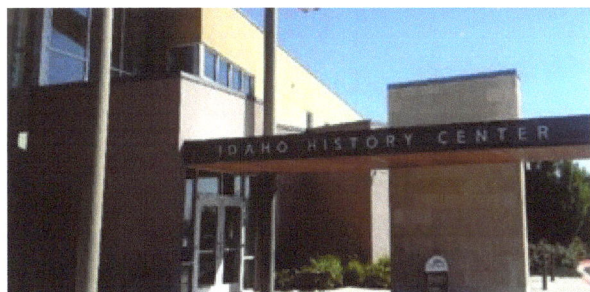

Figure 3. The Idaho State Historical Society Archives in Boise, 2012 (White).

these keywords mostly revealed urban renewal documents at Boise libraries. At archives and in special collections, these keywords led to the discovery of maps, photographs, and newspaper articles.

Documents from both public and private collections were used on this site. Resources were sought at the Albertsons Library at Boise State University, the Boise Public Library, the Idaho State Historic Preservation Office (SHPO), and Idaho State Historical Society Archives in Boise. Additional photographs and documents were generously provided by Lee Rice, II, John Bertram, and Pam Demo. Oral history interviews were recorded at the Idaho Black History Museum in Boise or at sites determined by the interviewee.

Data Digitization

The majority of this data had to be digitized in order to be displayed on the website. Archival documents were scanned with a flatbed scanner at 300dpi. Maps were scanned on a larger, high-resolution flatbed scanner. Photos and maps were converted into Joint Photographic Experts Group (JPG) files for the website and Tagged Image File Format (TIFF) files for use in ArcGIS and on the website. Photographs and video of the River Street Neighborhood were taken with a Nikon D5300 DSLR with an external shotgun microphone and with an iPhone 4s. In some instances, digital photographs of some articles and documents were also taken with the Nikon DSLR or the iPhone. Filtered video was taken on the iPhone using the 8mm app.

Oral history interviews were recorded with a Tascam DR-05 or similar quality recorder at 16-bit resolution. The resulting files were edited with Audacity.

Graphics and photos used on the website were edited using a variety of software. The original scans of the maps were, generally, too large for uploading to the website and were resized using Microsoft Paint or Pixlr.com. Photos that had been scanned as PDFs were edited and converted to JPGs using Microsoft Paint. Other graphics for the website and videos were created using Pixlr.com or ipiccy.com.

Maps of the River Street Neighborhood were created using ArcGIS 10.1 and were projected in WGS84, Zone 11, which is the same projection used in Google Earth. In order to get an idea of how the geography of the River Street Neighborhood changed over time, sections of the scanned maps were turned into TIFFs and were georectified as well as possible. The georectified files were turned into georeferenced TIFF format (geoTIFF) with 300dpi. Those geoTIFFs were exported as both Keyhole Markup Language (KML) layers so that they could be added to the website.

The geoTIFFs were also converted back to TIFFs and sequentially inserted into Microsoft PowerPoint in order to simulate a time-lapsed video of the geographic change in the neighborhood. This video was recorded as a Windows Media Video (WMV) file and edited with Microsoft Windows Movie Maker with the resulting video uploaded to YouTube.

Videos and screencasts were also created and edited using a variety of means. The introduction video was created by inserting photographs and video snippets into Animoto, a program that added and automated the transition graphics. Other videos were created using Windows Movie

Maker out of WMV or QuickTime (MOV) video files. The time-lapse map video and screencast were originally created in PowerPoint and saved as WMV files that were later edited in Movie Maker. The screencast was recorded using Open Broadcaster Software (OBS). Additional audio for the videos was recorded through OBS using a Logitech ClearChat stereo headset.

Since the videos were too large to host directly to the website, they were uploaded to YouTube and embedded in the site. PowerPoint presentations used on this website were uploaded to Slideshare.

The eBook draft documenting the River Street Digital History Project was created using a combination of Microsoft Word and PowerPoint. The final draft was professionally edited by Nicole Lavely and produced using Adobe InDesign. CreateSpace was used to publish paper copies of this book.

The River Street Digital History Project website was created on Wordpress.org and hosted with Bluehost. The Customizr template was used to format and display the website's materials.

Nearly all of the software used to create this site was free or inexpensive. The costly portions were covered by the Boise City Department of Arts and History grant. It is hoped that the River Street Digital History Project can be used as an example of how digital history can be done on a grass roots scale with near-professional results.

Figure 4. Recording screencasts with my daughter, Lydia White, 2014 (White).

History brought into the Digital Age
The River Street Digital Archive

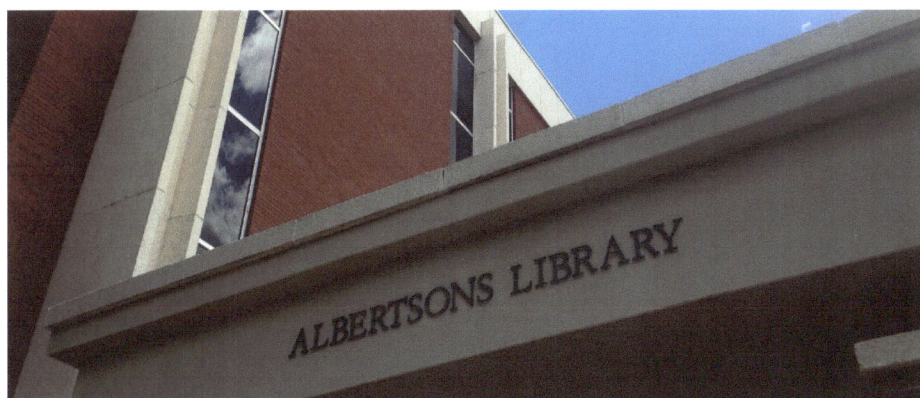

Figure 5. Albertsons Library at Boise State University, 2012 (White).

We've all heard stories from our grandparents and older relatives about the "Old Days." I sure do. I can recall sitting in the living room listening to my grandparents, great aunts, and great uncles talk about the way things used to be. How our families came to live where they do today, who's related to whom, and great deeds done in bygone days. I sat with rapt attention, hanging onto their every word–doing my best to imagine the setting of those stories, and in the process, painting pictures in my mind.

Today, my grandparents are gone. So are most of the patriarchs of my family. I can only remember portions of those tales, but the pictures remain, merely blurred by the passing of time. Wouldn't it be great if there was something to link the events in my relative's lives to my family in the present? A bit of the past that could connect my heritage with my life today? Wouldn't it be

even better if those links to the past were freely available on the internet for other people and communities around the world to access?

Some families have curated old photos and newspaper articles. These tidbits of the information help keep present generations grounded to their family's past. A few of these families have decided to donate these tangible resources to the various archives in communities around the country.

The River Street Digital History Project was conceived as a way for the residents of a historical community to make their memories and stories available to people around the world and to future generations. By turning historical photos, documents, and audio recordings into digital files that could be uploaded to the internet, some of the former residents of the River Street

Neighborhood in Boise, Idaho have made a portion of their lives available to the rest of the world. They have donated their memories and given the world an easily accessible way to enjoy them. We are all grateful for this generosity.

During the summer of 2014, a wealth of archival documents were digitized in preparation for their dissemination via this website. This website owes a debt of gratitude to the employees of the Idaho State Historic Archives in Boise, the Idaho State Historic Preservation Office, Special Collections at the Boise Public Library, and staff of the Albertsons Library at Boise State University who all helped make this project possible.

Bringing the archives to the world

Boise is host to a branch of the Idaho State Historical Society's Archives. At the archives in Boise, families from across the state have donated fragments of their past in order to be stored and maintained in perpetuity for future generations. In addition to receiving donations, the Idaho State Archives actively seeks out historical documents, photos, and other files to add to their collection. The archive is just one of the many ways people can access fragments of the past.

One of the best ways to commemorate the past is by talking with individuals about their histories and recording what they say. It is through direct conversations with the community elders that we have the chance to learn about the past from those who lived it. Historians and anthropologists who record these conversations call them oral histories or ethnographies. Sometimes these memories differ from the newspaper accounts curated in archives, but they are equally important because they provide different perspectives and can fill in the gaps between what was and was not written down.

Figure 6. Boise, Idaho taken from Table Rock, 1899 (courtesy of the Idaho State Historical Archive).

There is no right or wrong interpretation of the past. There are simply different perspectives. Oral histories contribute to a fuller, more diverse understanding of the past.

From Paper to Megabytes (archive)

Archival repositories do an excellent job of curating the tangible fragments of our past. They are sorely needed in our fast-paced, disposable world. But, the files housed in archives have some limits. One of the biggest hindrances is the fact that you physically have to go there to see their collections. For many people, the extra effort required to visit and the limited hours of many archives prevents local communities from fully harnessing their potential.

Digitizing archival collections is really the only way we can democratize this data and make it accessible to all. Sadly, the archives' staff are limited. Budgets for archival repositories are always precarious. Volunteers are frequently used to fill in staffing shortfalls and the paid staff spend most of their time inventorying collections and helping visiting researchers. Essentially, there is not enough manpower to digitize the whole of our archival collections.

The River Street Digital History Project attempted to convert all the existing archival data on the River Street Neighborhood into an easily accessible digital format that anyone with internet access can use. This work in one small corner of a mid-sized American town has brought a wealth of information within reach of people around the world. The wealth of data collected represents a small fraction of the total quantity of archival data that exists about Boise, Idaho and an even more miniscule portion of what we've collected about the history of the State of Idaho. It is almost too easy to say we need more projects like this one, but that is the truth. The wealth of archival data that exists in this country will remain in a marked box filed away in a building somewhere unless average Americans take the initiative to digitize the existing information about the places that count in their lives.

Visit www.riverstreethistory.com to read transcripts, see historical maps, and read newspaper articles about the River Street Neighborhood.

Building Upon a Firm Foundation of Previous Research
Previous River Street Projects

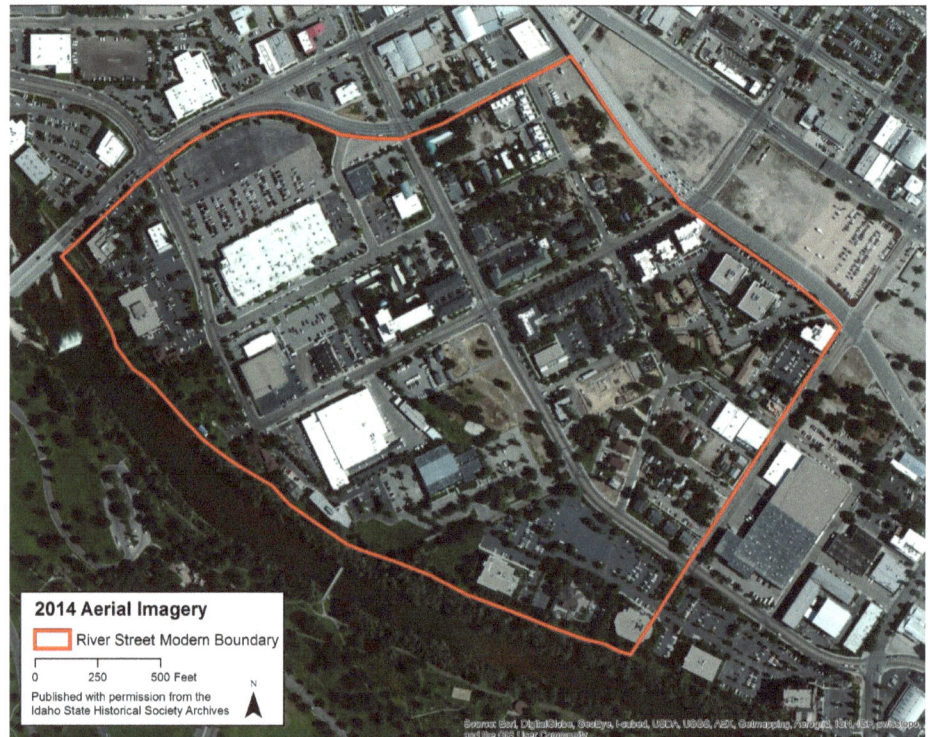

Figure 7. Overview of the River Street Neighborhood, 2014 (White).

The River Street Digital History Project is not the first time researchers have focused on this neighborhood. It was little mentioned in newspapers or Boise City studies prior to the 1960s, but, during the Urban Renewal boom, Boise planners focused several studies there. From the 1960s to the 1980s, River Street was the focus of several redevelopment schemes and, because it was zoned as industrial land, commercial development was encouraged. Newspaper articles from this time describe the various ways development was slowed in River Street and the fact that the neighborhood was considered "blighted" by the 1960s and 1970s. Of course, the people that lived in River Street saw things differently. They were more interested in gaining access to funding that would allow them to repair and rehabilitate the buildings in their community. Some research was conducted in the 1970s and 1980s that focused on figuring out ways to revive the community.

By the 1990s, research focused on preserving what was left of River Street. This work concentrated on documenting the remaining buildings and determining their historical value and it continues today.

Figure 8. (left) 609 Ash and 611 Ash
Figure 9. 611 Ash Street
Figure 10. 611 Ash Street, front elevation
Figure 11. 611 Ash Street, back elevation
Figure 12. 609 Ash Street
Figure 13. 609 Ash Street, front elevation
Figure 14. 609 Ash Street, side elevation
(Mateo Osa 1981, courtesy of the Idaho State Historical Archive)

Previous Studies

The River Street Neighborhood has been the subject of at least five historical research projects including an oral history project, a historic property inventory, a college class paper, and a graduate thesis. In 1981, Mateo Osa conducted oral history interviews with several African-American neighborhood residents with the intent of documenting the history of the Lee Street area in order to make recommendations for historic preservation. The interviews provided a background for the neighborhood from the perspective of its African-American residents and formed a baseline for what is known about the neighborhood's social dynamics.

Osa also documented 23 homes along Ash and Lee Streets. At the time (1980–1981), this was a relatively intact portion of the River Street Neighborhood that was being encroached upon by commercial development. Osa noted that it was one of the oldest, intact areas of Boise. The houses along Lee and Ash Streets were built with the anticipation that they would house working class Boiseans. This condition had not changed by the 1980s. Describing Lee Street in the early 1980s, Osa wrote:

"Lee Street is lined with mature trees and fences separate the yards from the sidewalks in front of the houses. Set in the midst of a warehouse and urban redevelopment district as it is, Lee Street stands out as an unique

Some of the photos taken by Osa can be found at the Idaho State Historical Archive.

Figure 15. 163 Ash Street, front elevation
Figure 16. 163 Ash Street, back elevation
(*Mateo Osa 1981, courtesty of the Idaho State Historical Archive*)
Figure 17. 1117 W Lee Street (White 2014)
Figure 18. 1120 W Lee Street
Figure 19. 1121 W Lee Street
Figure 20. 1127 W Lee Atreet
(White 2014)

and self-contained neighborhood. It deserves attention, not only as the traditional home of a segment of Boise's black community, but also as an area of virtually unaltered vernacular residential architecture. Also, noteworthy, is the degree of continuity in relationship to the rest of the community since, unlike many neighborhoods, it has not altered its basic character over the years but still provides basic low-income housing close to downtown."

Views of Lee and Ash Streets: 1981 and 2014

Lee Street is the only portion of the River Street Neighborhood that has been evaluated for its historical properties. Mateo Osa (1981) recommended this one-block area be saved from development because of its character as a historical residential district. Susan M. Stacy (1995) acknowledged the historicity of Lee Street, but stopped short of recommending it as a historical district. Many of the historical houses on this street remain.

Transcripts of the conversations recorded by Osa and photos of several inventoried houses are on file at the Idaho State Historical Society Archives in Boise. The text of his final report "Survey of Lee Street Neighborhood" is on file at the Idaho State Historic Preservation Office also in Boise. You can download a partial copy of Osa's report at www.riverstreethistory.com; however, the names and addresses of Osa's informants and details of the private properties surveyed have been redacted.

The River Street Area Survey was conducted in 1995 to evaluate neighborhood buildings under Section 106 of the National Historic Preservation Act (NHPA). A continuation of the effort to preserve buildings in the neighborhood that was initiated by Osa, this report **River Street Area Reconnaissance Survey (1995)** (Idaho Historic Properties Survey Report No.

222), was conducted and written by Susan M. Stacy. The survey was prepared for the Boise City Historic Preservation Commission and covered an area of 300 acres. The survey evaluated 151 buildings between Americana Blvd. on the west, Broadway Blvd. on the east, W. Myrtle Street on the north, and the Boise River on the south. This evaluation failed to create a historic preservation district within River Street. Stacy explains that the neighborhoods south of Myrtle between Broadway Blvd. and Sixteenth St. (Americana Blvd.) were mature by 1915 and were largely dedicated to house working class Boiseans (1995:9). In the years between World War I and II, a warehouse district developed along the railroad tracks between Ninth and Sixth Streets. This district continued expanding for the next few decades, consuming many previously residential properties. World War II saw an influx of residents to this area, given the fact that it was largely rental properties and was one of the few places African Americans were allowed to rent in Boise. River Street was occupied by a large number of African American soldiers and their families at that time; however, most moved away following the war. The 1960s ushered in a period or urban renewal and Boise City officials and planners sought various ways

Figure 21. 511 S. 11th Street, 2012 (White).

to redevelop River Street, as it was considered a blight on the city's landscape. Many residential dwellings in the neighborhood were destroyed at this time, although most of the urban renewal in Boise focused on blocks in downtown Boise.

Stacy's inventory provided preservation recommendations, although she did not conduct exhaustive research on each and every property evaluated. Her report states that the River Street Neighborhood was unique because of its identity as Boise's black neighborhood and acknowledges Osa's recommendation to preserve the Lee and Ash Street portion of the neighborhood. Stacy writes (1995:13-14):

> **"About 1980–1982 the Idaho State Historic Preservation Office undertook a survey of the "Lee Street Historic District," [Osa 1981] 22 houses located on Lee and Ash Streets. The survey analyst and the SHPO office concluded that the area was eligible for nomination to the National Register of Historic Places. When Boise City objected to this conclusion, the survey and report were sent to the National Park Service (NPS). The NPS agreed with the SHPO and issued a formal determination that the district was eligible. The significance of this decision is that any agency proposing to impact the area adversely and use federal funds to do so (such as Boise City Community Development Block Grants or other federal resources) will be obliged to mitigate such impacts according to a plan negotiated with the SHPO. This requirement derives from Section 106 of the National Historic Preservation Act."**

Stacy continues to state that the Lee and Ash Street area remained (in 1995) one of the few places in River Street where older homes were still standing. She recommended that other historic houses be moved to the Lee and Ash area to fill in vacant lots, which would strengthen the likelihood of preserving the place as a historic district.

Also in 1995, a student paper titled "The River Street Neighborhood" was written by Jeffrey D. Johns for the History Department at Boise State University (Johns 1995). This work was another continuation of research pioneered by Osa and provided an improved historic context for the Lee and Ash Street area. Johns' discussion of the effects of urban renewal on River Street and his systematic inventory of the houses along these streets are useful updates to the 1981 inventory. A copy of Johns' paper is on file at the Idaho State Historical Society Archives in Boise.

The seminal work on the River Street Neighborhood was published in 2006 as a Master's thesis. In 2006, Pam Demo wrote "Boise's River Street Neighborhood: Lee, Ash, and Lovers Lane/Pioneer Streets: The South Side of the Tracks" as part of her Master's Degree in Anthropology for the University of Idaho. This thesis focused on the architectural history and social environment of Lee and Ash Streets and is the culmination of over 30 years of research in this section of River Street. Demo brought together the existing data on the neighborhood and integrated Osa's oral histories, Stacy's and Johns' building surveys, and other historic resources into her rich recollection of life in River Street. Acknowledging the dynamism and diversity of River Street's historical population, Demo writes:

> "Residents who arrived poor, were of color, or spoke no English, left when they could afford to and others moved in to take their place. Some stayed in the neighborhood finding security, friendship, and a sense of community. They invested in their homes, raising families, and by their continued presence they contributed to the social fabric that connected streets and neighbors."

Demo's thesis is housed at the University of Idaho's library. She has also been known to distribute PDF versions by request.

Other River Street Digital History Projects

In addition to these documents, other websites discuss the digital history of River Street. In 2011, the website River Street Neighborhood: Changes in the Physical and Cultural Landscape 1863-1970 (www.riverstreethistory.wordpress.

Figure 22. The River Street Neighborhood on the Boise 150 Virtual Tour, at www.boiseartsandhistory.org/remnants-of-boise/index.html (2014).

com) was created by students of a Public History class at Boise State University. This website provides an excellent description of the way River Street's landscape has changed since the 1860s.

Portions of the River Street Neighborhood are included in the visually stunning Boise 150 virtual tour, Remnants of Boise (www.boiseartsandhistory.org/remnants-of-boise/index.html). This project was sponsored by the Boise City Department of Arts and History and the virtual tour includes places in the River Street Neighborhood including Lee Street.

Urban Renewal Studies on River Street

What to do with River Street? This has been a lingering question in the minds of Boise planners for decades. Beginning in the 1960s, the City of Boise began conducting urban renewal studies in order to investigate the effects of demolishing older buildings in downtown Boise and constructing new ones in their place. Initially, the focus of this renewal was a huge swath of downtown Boise north of Myrtle Street. Buildings in this part of downtown Boise were old and began showing their age. The city's growth was increasingly oriented toward the suburbs by this time as well. Investment in old downtown was waning. The city was looking for ways they could encourage growth in Boise's aging core.

Urban Renewal was part of a nationwide campaign in most major cities in the United States between the 1950s and 1970s. The central tenet of Urban Renewal was: Stimulate growth by tearing down old buildings and replacing them with new ones. But, before the old buildings were torn down, cities like Boise conducted feasibility studies that would provide an idea as to what the impacts would be after the

existing buildings were torn down. Public meetings accompanied these studies and, in most communities, historic preservation and social justice advocates fought against urban renewal. This is, generally, how the urban renewal process went in Boise and it mirrors events taking place across the U.S. at this time.

While the initial studies focused on Boise's downtown core, city officials soon set their sights on the River Street Neighborhood. Redevelopment studies on River Street were initiated during the 1970s and continue to this day. Below is a sample of the many urban development plans conducted on the River Street area. You can read the reports at www.riverstreethistory.com.

---

n.d. *River Street Neighborhood Plan: A Comparison of the Neighborhood Development Project and the River Street Design Center Plan.* **Document on file at the Boise Public Library.**

Although this short report has no date, it must have been published sometime around 1975. This report summarizes the Boise Redevelopment Agency (BRA) and the River Street Community Design Center plans. The BRA plan was criticized because it failed to adequately take low-income and minority interests into account. This report concludes by recommending: the maximization of investments in public utilities, curtailing sprawl, saving open spaces (parks and the Greenbelt), encouraging the creation of low-income housing, and adopting a transportation policy that promotes neighborhood cohesiveness.

Bertram, John and Pat Walsh
1973 *River Street Neighborhood Plan.* **River Street Community Design Center, Boise.**

The River Street Neighborhood Plan was co-authored by River Street resident and long-time Boisean John Bertram (you can see a summary of

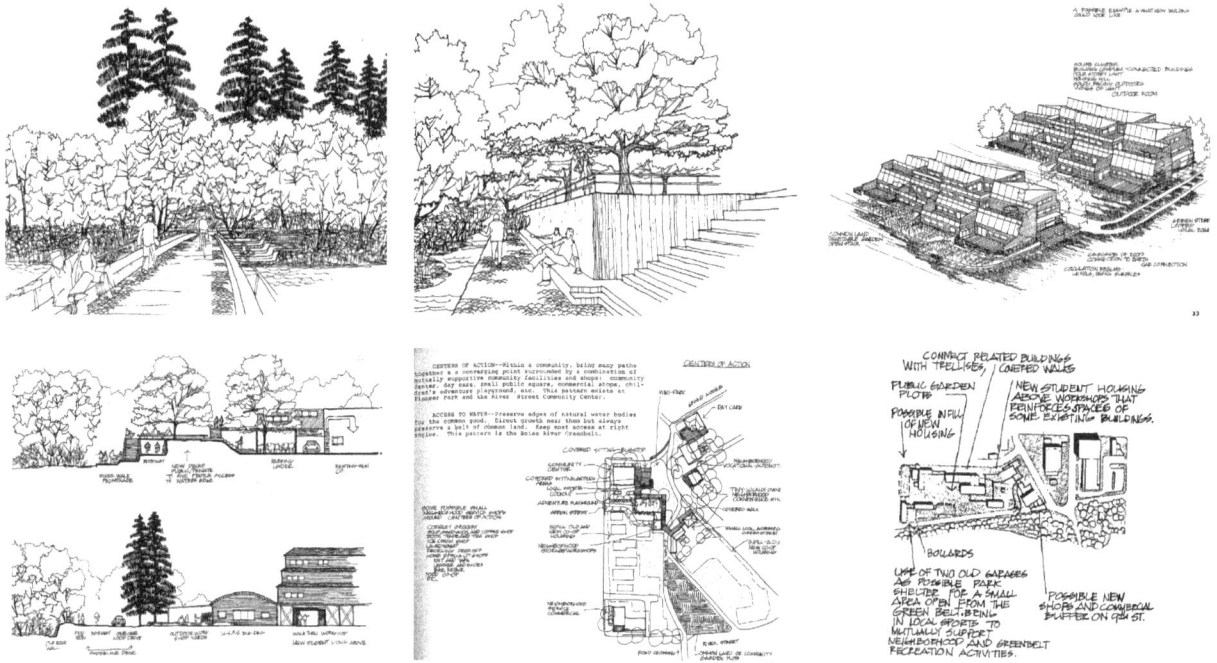

Figure 23. Brian McCarter's *A Rebuilding Process for River Street Neighborhood, Boise, Idaho,* 1975 (Albertsons Library, Boise State University).

John Bertram's 2014 oral history interview here). This study covered the boundaries of the greater River Street Neighborhood, which extended as far east as Capitol Blvd. This study area also included the remaining residential area of the neighborhood and the warehouse district that exists to the east (the 8th Street Marketplace and Boise Public Library area today). This was the most extensive report published on the neighborhood at that time and it made several recommendations that have actually come to pass. For instance, the authors suggested that the city should complete the Greenbelt along the Boise River, transform the warehouses along Eighth Street into a historical commercial district, construct a new public library along Capitol Blvd., and facilitate low-income housing in the River Street neighborhood. The neglect of buildings in the neighborhood was cited as a public concern and the study suggested that the city should help revitalize homes in the area. Based on what has happened to this area since the creation of this report, it is safe to say

that this report truly helped guide development in the River Street Neighborhood.

McCarter, Brian
1975 *A Rebuilding Process for River Street Neighborhood, Boise, Idaho.* University of Oregon, Eugene. Document on file at the Albertsons Library, Boise State University, Boise.

Just like Bertram and Walsh, McCarter recognized the true value of the River Street Neighborhood to developers was the fact that it was a residential district adjacent to downtown Boise and the Boise River. McCarter's vision for River Street included transforming the riverbank into an attractive park (the Greenbelt) and adding higher density housing to the existing housing stock. His ultimate goal for River Street was the creation of a mixed-use neighborhood with recreation and commercial venues located within walking distance from a variety of low to moderate-density residential options.

The scenario envisioned by McCarter can

be seen through the forward-thinking drawings he created of this redevelopment project. Some of the elements of his plan have actually been completed, such as the Greenbelt, the construction of commercial offices along the Boise River, and the addition of higher density residential structures.

Capitol City Development Corporation (CCDC) 2003 *Pioneer Corridor Design Competition.* Capitol City Development Corporation, Boise. Document provided by Pam Demo, Boise. Also available on the CCDC website: http://www.ccdcboise.com/

The Capitol City Development Corporation (CCDC) has emerged as a major player in the development/redevelopment of the River Street Neighborhood. One of its goals is to transform the neighborhood into an attractive, livable place, and the creation of quality public amenities is one strategy they have been employing. Transforming Pioneer Street (formerly Lovers Lane) into a pedestrian pathway has been promoted as a way the city can improve the attractiveness of River Street. In 2003, the CCDC held a design competition to determine how the Pioneer Pathway would become a reality.

Capitol City Development Corporation (CCDC) 2004 *River Street-Myrtle Street Master Plan.* Capitol City Development Corporation, Boise. Document provided by Pam Demo, Boise. Also available on the CCDC website: http://www.ccdcboise.com/

By the early 2000s, the River Street Neighborhood had been the focus of development/redevelopment plans for about 30 years. Several of the previously mentioned ideas had come to fruition by that time including the completion of the Greenbelt, establishment of the Boise Public Library in its present location, the adaptive reuse of the 8th Street Marketplace, and the construction of commercial offices south of River Street (a topic discussed in newspaper articles from the 1980s). While low-income housing had been emphasized in the 1970s studies, transforming River Street into a flourishing urban neighborhood with a mix of shopping and recreation options became the goal for 2025. The CCDC has been hard at work to accomplish one of the goals outlined in the 1970s studies: Building the Pioneer Walkway into an inviting pedestrian avenue that can be used for transportation and recreation.

Figure 24. Today's Pioneer Walkway follows the route of Lover's Lane, 2014 (White).

Keyser Marston Associates, Inc.
2004 *Economic Feasibility of the First Amended and Restated River-Myrtle/Old Boise Urban Renewal District.* **Prepared for the Capitol City Development Corporation, Boise. Keyser Marston Associates, Inc., Los Angeles.**

In order to accomplish the desired redevelopment goals, the CCDC had to calculate how much it would cost and the means by which to pay for it. NOTE: This was published before the recession, consequently these numbers may not be accurate anymore.

Capitol City Development Corporation (CCDC)
2005 *Capitol City Development Corporation Annual Report.* **Capitol City Development Corporation, Boise. Document provided by Pam Demo, Boise.**

The Pioneer Walkway and the Smart City Initiative/Creative Cities are highlighted as among the CCDC's 2004 successes. Smart Cities was created in 2000 to foster a more livable community that could lure creative businesses and professional to Boise. Recent research conducted by the Seattle Green Lab has demonstrated that historical neighborhoods like River Street are more amenable to creative professionals and have the potential to transform cities into creative centers.

The quest to redevelop the River Street Neighborhood continues today, as do attempts to preserve physical traces of its history. Fortunately, recent research has confirmed that historic places like River Street are more beneficial to cities than destroying old buildings to make way for new ones. In 2014, the Seattle Green Lab, a unit of the National Trust for Historic Preservation, published the report, ***Older, Smaller, Better: Measuring how the character of buildings and blocks influences***

urban vitality. Their research concluded that: "All across America, blocks of older, smaller buildings are quietly contributing to robust local economies and distinctive livable communities." The authors continue by demonstrating that older blocks have more active communities, contain a higher number of jobs per square foot, and host a greater density of minority and women-owned businesses. Basically, older places like the River Street Neighborhood are essential to the vitality and vibrancy of Boise's community. You can download a free copy of this report at www.preservationnation.org.

The History of River Street

"The Negro in the history of the Pacific Northwest is indeed a bold subject when it is realized that there are so few Negroes in that section of the United States even at the present day, and in the early history of the section there were even fewer than now" (Savage 1928).

African Americans comprise a small percentage of Idaho's population today. Currently, African Americans make up only about 1.5% of Boise's population, which means the black population in town is greater today (2014) than it has ever been. Black people were never the largest racial group in the River Street either, but they were the neighborhood's most emblematic residents. For decades, River Street has been known as "the Black Neighborhood"—the place where black people lived. The aggregation of Boise's black people in River Street was the result of discriminatory housing mores that made them unwelcome elsewhere in the city.

It is important to note, however, that African Americans have been present in what is now Boise, Idaho for almost as long as Euroamericans have. It is even more important to note that, long before black or white populations lived in the area that is now River Street, it was inhabited by Native Americans; specifically, members of the Shoshone Tribe.

Long Before River Street

It should be no surprise to realize that everywhere human beings live today, they have already lived for thousands of years. The River Street area is no different. Long before Europeans arrived, the area that would become Boise, Idaho was occupied by Native Americans. Archaeological evidence recovered at Wilson Butte Cave indicates human beings were living in southern Idaho more than 11,000 years ago and have continued to live there ever since (Walker 1978). Southern Idaho was much colder and wetter than it is today. People at that time primarily hunted big game animals that are extinct in southern Idaho today: mammoth, ground sloths, and bison.

Around 8,000 years ago, the climate in southern Idaho started to change. It became dryer and hotter. The large glaciers that never covered southern Idaho but covered parts of northern Idaho began to recede. The population in southern Idaho grew and the archaeological remains of two different lifeways have been recovered: The people in southeastern Idaho adapted to the desert lifestyle while folks to the east continued relying on bison herds. Archaeologists believe these two archaeological cultures are the descendants of the Northern Shoshone (Walker 1987). The Boise area was historically occupied by the western band of the Northern Shoshone.

By the time Europeans started recording the Native American way of life in southern Idaho, they had been living there for hundreds of generations and had adapted to their arid, Great

Basin home. The Northern Shoshone lived in an area that extended from eastern Oregon into Wyoming and south into Nevada. Combining both Great Basin and plateau cultural characteristics, the Shoshone lived in small bands subsisting on seeds, pine nuts, wild wheat, bitterroot, and camas. They also fished for salmon, conducted communal rabbit, sage hen, and antelope drives, and hunted for other game as it was available. Their mobility was greatly increased after obtaining horses in the late sixteenth century and the Shoshone people began expanding onto the northern Great Plains. The horse also gave the Shoshone additional options to their seasonal subsistence cycle. Groups east of the Boise River intensified their reliance on buffalo while Shoshone in the Boise area continued to focus on salmon runs because these supplies were adequate to meet their needs (Heaton 2005; Walker 1978).

The Arrival of the Euroamericans

Fur trappers were the first to encounter the Shoshone in Idaho. Lewis and Clark encountered a Shoshone band in the Lemhi Valley in 1805 and, during the 1810s and 1830s, fur trappers maintained a light but steady presence in southwestern Idaho. In 1834, the Hudson's Bay Company built the first Fort Boise at the confluence of the Boise and Snake Rivers near present day Weiser and Nathaniel J. Wyeth founded Fort Hall on the Snake River. This was the first sustained non-Native presence in Shoshone territory in Idaho (Heaton 2005; Wells 2000:24–25).

The establishment of the Oregon Trail across Idaho brought thousands of Euroamericans into Shoshone territory and sparked conflict. During the 1840s, 1850s, and 1860s, tens of thousands of stock animals grazed on Shoshone lands and thousands of emigrants appropriated water, timber, and other resources without permission or paying for their use. Intermittent attacks on these emigrants brought calls for the United States government to intervene (Madsen 1980:27–29). The 1863 Organic Act that created the Idaho Territory also brought the first Indian Agents to southern Idaho and ushered in an era of treaties. In 1864, a treaty was negotiated with Shoshone living along the Boise River where the Shoshone agreed to give up title to all lands within 30 miles on each side of the river, including the area that would become Boise City (Madsen 1980:43). Fort Boise was relocated to the Boise City area in 1863 due to increased hostilities from the Shoshone in the Boise Basin cause by gold rushers and the fact that the original fort near Weiser had been abandoned in 1854. The horrible conditions they faced due to the loss of their most productive lands at the hands of Euroamericans further inflamed Shoshone aggression, but they were unable to dislodge these newcomers from their traditional lands. In 1869, the Shoshone living near Boise were relocated to the Fort Hall Reservation (Madsen 1980:43–54).

While no archaeological evidence of Native Americans has been identified in the River Street Neighborhood, this location was probably very important to the Shoshone and their ancestors given its proximity to the Boise River and the longevity of these traditional people in the area.

From Fortress to Town

In 1862, a small party of Euroamericans made the arduous trek from the former site of Old Fort Boise near present-day Weiser to the Boise Basin near Idaho City, where they searched for gold. They found what they were looking for in August of that year.

The discovery of gold in the Boise Basin sparked a rush that brought people surging into the area. Mining camps popped up throughout the area in 1862–1863. By the summer of 1863, an estimated 15,000–20,000 non-Native Americans had emigrated to the Basin. Roads soon snaked into the Basin and small towns were forged. Idaho City was founded in 1862 and an assay office was built in Boise City to count all the gold pouring down from the hills (Bird 1934). Despite this surge, the Boise Basin gold fields were not open to all. Boise County passed a law in 1863 excluding African Americans and Chinese from prospecting. These laws did not stop all black miners, who continued to enter Idaho's gold fields throughout the 1860s and 1870s, but they did deter many (Bird 1934:119; Mercier and Simon-Smolinski 1990:4–6).

By the 1870s, the Boise Basin was panning out. Cities that provided supplies to the miners like Boise and Walla Walla fared much better than towns founded in the gold fields. The gold rush had brought enough people that the Idaho Territory was founded in 1863. Fort Boise was founded that year in its present location to protect miners and Oregon Trail travelers. Under much controversy, the territorial capitol was established at Boise in 1864 (Bird 1934:175). Steady growth occurred in Boise City during the rest of the 1860s and 1870s as land was cleared, irrigation ditches constructed, and agricultural fields planted. Log cabins gave way to frame buildings. Churches, schools, and substantial brick buildings were slowly built. By 1880, the town's population had reached nearly 1,900 individuals.

"Can't you hear the whistle blowing?": The Railroad and River Street

Whispers of a railroad arriving in Boise began during the 1860s, but reached a crescendo during the late 1880s. Construction of the Oregon Short Line (OSL) Railroad across southern Idaho began in 1883 and, while several routes had been proposed, the line would not pass through Boise. The town's citizens remained hopeful. Talk of constructing a line from Nampa to Boise began. An 1885 Boise City map depicts a "Railroad Reserve" along the southern edge of downtown Boise. Thoughtful land owners and speculators moved in to grab land before the railroad was a reality. Boise gained rail access when the Idaho Central Railway completed a spur track to Boise in 1887, but the Oregon Short Line mainline would not reach the city until 1925 (Bird 1934:252–253; Waite nd:6).

The 1890s brought real estate speculation and development schemes to the area that would become the River Street Neighborhood. John McClellan started this process when he platted

Figure 25. View of Boise from Table Rock (1899) (courtesy of the Idaho State Historical Archive).

Figure 26. John McClellan was one of the original residents of what would become River Street (n.d.) (courtesy of the Idaho State Historical Archive).

Figure 27. "1863" is carved on the front of McClellan's cabin (n.d.) (Ibid.).

his property in 1890. During the 1890s, the Riverside, Miller, and City Park Additions were platted in anticipation of the arrival of the Oregon Short Line Railroad. The River Street area was subdivided to provide parcels for warehouses and housing. It was envisioned that this would become a home for the workers employed at the various warehouses that flanked the railroad and businesses in downtown Boise. Few opulent houses were built in the area (Demo 2006; Stacy 1995).

By the 1900s, the River Street Neighborhood had evolved into a mixture of commercial and residential properties. Idaho became a state in 1890 and Boise was poised for growth. The town had nearly 6,000 residents and the construction of the New York Canal provided an infusion of farming opportunities brought by people and money (Stacy 1995:7). The majority of houses in River Street were built between 1900 and 1930 (Demo 2006). Historical maps show that the completion of the Ridenbaugh Canal in 1878 and Diversion Dam in 1909 for the New York Canal had greatly diminished the Boise River's flow near River Street, but seasonal floods were still common and the land adjacent to the river would remain undeveloped for decades to come.

A Place to Live South of the Railroad Tracks

The River Street Neighborhood was carved from the riparian cottonwood forests that flanked the Boise River during the 1890s and early 1900s. It was a place where real estate speculation resulted in the creation of a neighborhood and community:

Riverside Park

Located near the present-day intersection of River Street and 9th Street, Riverside Park opened in 1902 and provided an attractive and convenient place for Boiseans to relax and enjoy the amusements. The park featured a bandstand, dance pavilion, theater and baseball field. While dances were frequent draws to the park, the baseball field and theater hosted some of the most memorable events. In the wake of the 1906 San Francisco Earthquake, the San Francisco Opera Company performed at Riverside Park until a new venue could be secured back in San Francisco. The baseball field was home to several Boise teams and some of Boise's most memorable games took place there.

Riverside Park remained open until 1912. Its location was mostly covered with warehouses during the early twentieth century, but portions of the park also became part of a Girl Scout camp and a Forest Service office that used to occupy the land between River Street and the Boise River west of Capitol Boulevard. Former residents recall playing at the Girl Scout grounds, which featured a softball field, into the 1960s.

Visit www.riverstreethistory.com to hear more about the recreational activities of River Street residents.

The seeds for a neighborhood at River Street had been sown during the first decades of the twentieth century. These seeds would mature in the years to come.

South Side of the Tracks Becomes A Community

River Street has always been slated for development. From its earliest days, real estate speculation was central to this location as a vehicle for expanding downtown Boise. The arrival of the Oregon Short Line Railroad launched development in this section of Boise. The initial land owners, including John McClellan, subdivided and platted this area in hopes that the railroad would spur construction. During the first half of the twentieth century, a collection of residential houses were built along the streets between the railroad tracks on the north, River Street on the south, Sixteenth Street (present day Americana Boulevard) on the north, and Tenth Street on the east. Warehouses occupied the area east of Tenth Street all the way to what is now Capitol Boulevard.

Figure 28. The old Union Pacific Depot near River Street brought passengers from far and wide to Boise (n.d.) (courtesy of the Idaho State Historical Archive)
Figure 29. During the early 20th century, locomotives like this one brought passengers to Boise (1907) (Ibid.)
Figure 30. The Oregon Short Line Railroad roundhouse was just northwest of the River Street Neighborhood (n.d.) (Ibid.)
Figure 31. Riverside Park was one of River Street's finest amenities during the early 20th century (n.d.) (Ibid.)
Figure 32. A view of the bandshell at Riverside Park (n.d.) (Ibid.)
Figure 33. A 1902 advertisement for a baseball game at Riverside Park, Boise, Idaho (Ibid.).

SUNDAY
BALL GAME
Aug. 3 Only.
New England Bloomers
VS.
Riverside Park
The Eastern Girls against the Western Boys in a red hot game.
The Bloomers' famous pitcher Miss Grace Wood, will positively appear in the box.

By the Roaring Twenties, the River Street Neighborhood was poised for growth. It was filled with relatively new housing stock. The number of warehouses along the "spur" were expanding, which provided jobs for local residents and commerce for the city. The population of Boise was rapidly growing. Between 1900 and 1920, Boise had grown from approximately 6,000 residents to over 21,000. River Street remained a working-class neighborhood with Basque and European immigrant populations. The first African Americans also moved in at this time. River Street and Boise City were on the upswing.

The pendulum had gone the other way by the 1970s. While Boise's population was rapidly increasing in 1970, growth had stalled during the 1960s. Suburban expansion across open desert and former farmland was absorbing most of the population growth. New people living in new houses wanted new shopping malls. Older buildings in downtown Boise were decaying and many of the houses in River Street were over 50 years old. Many of the absentee property owners in River Street had let their rentals decline, and Boise city officials saw the neighborhood as an eyesore. Crime crept into the neighborhood and the Civil Rights Movement abolished the real estate restrictions that had kept African Americans and other non-whites from leaving the neighborhood. Those that could afford to left River Street. The City's solution to this decay was urban renewal. Essentially, Boise had to decide whether to rehabilitate older buildings in the urban core or demolish them and build something new.

River Street traversed a turbulent period during the mid-twentieth century and, by the 1970s, much of what once was had been lost. Houses had been demolished. Businesses shuttered. New, large condominiums and apartments were built on top of the previous small, detached, single-family dwellings. Attempts at historic preservation had failed. The future of the River Street Neighborhood was not clear, but one constant throughout all these changes was community.

River Street during the War Years

Most of the houses in the River Street Neighborhood were constructed during the 1900s, 1910s, and 1920s (Demo 2006). Most of these buildings were intended from their construction to be rented out and consisted of a range of "ready-built" houses—standard dwellings that were made in factories and shipped on railroad cars to a town where they were assembled based on enclosed instructions. Demo (2006:32) explains:

> **"By the early 1900s, the grandiose architectural plans for 'cottage' and 'bungalow' were scaled down by enterprising home-building companies as they responded to huge demands for affordable, quality housing from a growing American working-class that was more than willing to settle for small, uncomplicated, and unadorned homes."**

During the first decades of the twentieth century, companies compiled plan books where potential homebuyers could select plans for their homes from large catalogs they would like to buy. The materials for the selected home were delivered to the lot where it was to be erected and workmen or the home owner assembled the house based on instructions that came with the house kit.

At the same time when residential buildings were being added to the neighborhood, warehouses and commercial buildings were also being built along the railroad tracks. The neighborhood was zoned as "unrestricted" in 1928, which meant the existing residential buildings would remain but industrial and commercial growth could continue on all sides (Osa 1982:2; Stacy 1995:9). This zoning immediately diminished the desirability of the neighborhood. Those homeowners that lived in the neighborhood started moving away, either renting out their homes or selling them outright.

Around this time, the arrival of more European immigrants and non-Euroamericans to the neighborhood increased. The first Basque immigrants arrived in the neighborhood in 1902 and were followed by a few more Basque families and shepherding bachelors during the 1910s. Most of the Basque congregated around Lee and Ash Streets and on Lover's Lane (Demo 2006:105–106). European immigrants from other countries also arrived during the first decades of the twentieth century: most notably Greek and Croatian individuals and families (Demo 2006; 108–109). Immigrants faced discrimination outside the neighborhood and were increasingly forced into the River Street area. Within the neighborhood, however, people were friendly, helpful, and neighborly.

World War II brought a large number of African American soldiers to the military bases near Boise: Gowen Field and Mountain Home Air Force Base. Many of these black soldiers were allowed to bring their families, but faced few housing options in Boise. River Street was the only place they were allowed to rent homes (Osa 1982:5; Stewart 1980), as well as the only area that African Americans could buy homes, which contrasted with other parts of the country where blacks were not allowed to buy property at all. Long-time African American River Street resident Bessie Stewart recalls convincing her husband to purchase a house in the neighborhood. They immediately rented it out to black soldiers with families and didn't move into the home until after World War II (Stewart 1980). The Stewarts were not alone. A number of other black Boiseans bought homes in the River Street Neighborhood. Many of these individuals lived in River Street for decades.

Decline: the 1960s and 1970s
After World War II, the surge of black renters

Figure 34. The intersection of Lee and Ash Streets is in the heart of the River Street Neighborhood, 2014 (White).

in the River Street Neighborhood subsided but it remained a predominately rental neighborhood. The neighborhood demographics changed sharply during the 1960s when African Americans in Boise began pushing for their civil rights. African American activist Dorothy Buckner recalls that the push for civil rights was spearheaded by a small part of Boise's black community. Most blacks were against upsetting the status quo even though they were excluded from living in most of the city. There was discrimination in Boise, but it was not even close to the way things were in other parts of the United States (Buckner 1981). Boise's schools were integrated. African Americans were allowed to own businesses and homes. Violent racism was rare. For most blacks, the environment was not great but it was good enough.

In the 1960s, a number of civil rights marches were held in Boise and representatives from the NAACP and Urban League conducted studies and held public meetings to discuss the status of African Americans in the city. African Americans were no longer restricted to living in River Street after the Civil Rights Act of 1968 and, similar to the effects of the 1928 zoning

of the neighborhood, many of those who could moved away from the neighborhood.

During the mid-twentieth century, the River Street Neighborhood also became known for illicit activity. Illegal activity that had previously been centered in downtown Boise appears to have expanded into the River Street Neighborhood and certain parts of the neighborhood became known for gambling and prostitution. Residents continually say that this type of activity was concentrated around Pioneer Street/Lover's Lane (today's Pioneer Walkway). Nevertheless, Boiseans began to view the entire neighborhood as a place of vice.

Interviews with former residents have acknowledged the presence of illicit activity on Pioneer Street (Buckner 1981, Madry 2014, Terrell 2014). Several of the businesses on Pioneer had legitimate business street fronts while the back of the shop housed gambling and other activities. One example is the Blackjack Barbeque Restaurant that used to operate at 500 S. Ash Street. Today, this is a neighborhood center but, according to Dorothy Buckner (1981), it doubled as a gambling hall. Blackjack's was operated by African

Figure 35. The former Blackjack's Barbeque building is a community center today, 2014 (White).

American entrepreneur "Pistol" Johnson. In addition to operating the barbeque restaurant, Johnson also repaired houses in the neighborhood and acted as a rental agent and property manager for absentee property owners in River Street (Buckner 1981).

The tales of Pioneer Street as a red light/gambling district are widely known in Boise lore, but residents have always wanted to stress that River Street was much more than a place to have a good time. It was a close-knit community where residents overlooked skin color and judged each other based on the content of their character.

Urban Renewal: From the 1970s to the Present

While downtown Boise's current state is the culmination of both historic preservation efforts and Urban Renewal, River Street has remained at a crossroads for over 50 years. On one hand, development agencies and real estate developers would like to see it transformed into high-density urban living. On the other hand, social justice and historic preservation interests want River Street to become a mixed-use district that serves the needs of low-income Boiseans while preserving what's left of one of the city's oldest neighborhoods.

The urban renewal movement in Boise started in the 1960s with studies conducted by the Boise Planning and Development Committee. Initially, the committee targeted a portion of downtown Boise between Front, Washington, 12th and 3rd Streets. This area surrounded the Idaho Capitol building and consisted of older buildings, some of which had not been maintained. As previously mentioned, Boise planners and officials felt that demolishing these buildings and constructing new ones in their place would attract new investment and businesses.

The City of Boise entertained a number of development projects in downtown Boise during the 1970s including the construction of a mall and a conference center, the latter of which was actually built. A large number of buildings dating to the nineteenth century were demolished in the process.

Planners also set their sights on the River Street Neighborhood at that time because of its reputation as a place of ill-repute and the large number of neglected rental properties. Feasibility studies were conducted at this time in order to decide what to do about the neighborhood. During the 1980s and 1990s, a number of high-density residential buildings were built in the heart of the neighborhood. The floodplain of the Boise River south of River Street was finally developed during the 1980s.

Historic preservation studies were also conducted at this time and preservation was recommended for portions of the neighborhood.

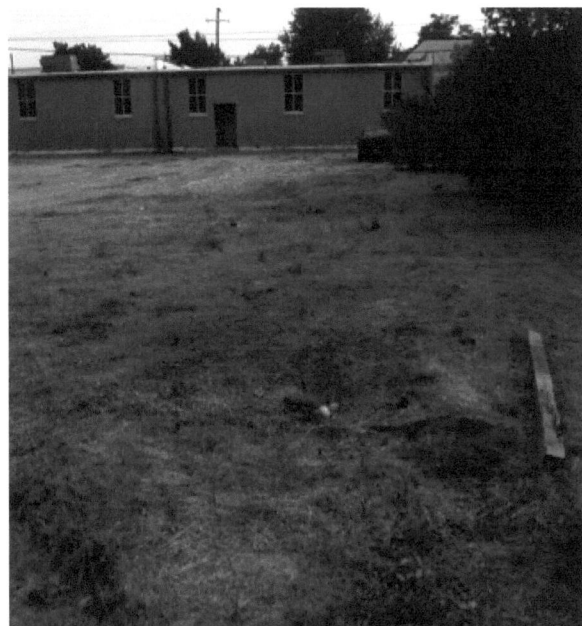

Figure 36. This vacant lot on Lee Street awaits development, 2012 (White).

To date, these recommendations have largely not been heeded.

The result of this dialectic between development and preservation has stunted the development of the neighborhood. It is neither a historical district nor a high-density, urban enclave. Recently, several property owners have begun repairing the historical homes that remain while multi-family apartment and condominiums have also been established. Today, River Street is an eclectic place that has the potential to become a pleasingly quirky central neighborhood in downtown Boise—a livable place at the heart of a vibrant community.

> Visit www.riverstreethistory.com to learn more about the effects of Urban Renewal and see studies conducted on the River Street Neighborhood.

River Street as a Community

The River Street Neighborhood has always been a multi-ethnic community. From the European immigrants of the 1910s to the African immigrants that live there today, life in the neighborhood has always been characterized as hospitable. Interviews with former residents highlight this fact.

African Americans in the neighborhood were close, but they also had good Euroamerican friends who were willing to lend a helping hand whenever necessary. Doris Thomas recalls that people of all races made homes and founded businesses in the neighborhood. Businesses in River Street, such as Zurcher's and Pearl Grocery, did not discriminate. Residents of all races were welcome to come in and shop. Ellen Perkins and Erma Hayman lived in River Street for decades and, even though they were black and came to the neighborhood during the height of discrimination, were able to own homes. When Perkins' husband passed away,

Figure 37. The former Zurcher's Grocery is still a River Street fixture, n.d. (courtesy of the Idaho State Historical Archive).

she recalls Euroamerican neighbors coming over immediately to offer a helping hand. Other former residents recall playing with neighborhood children of all races. Many of these friendships even continued while attending schools located outside the neighborhood.

John Bertram moved to River Street during the 1970s as a young man. He was attracted to the place because of the plight of its low-income residents and decided this was the place where he would work toward improving. He bought a house, a fixer-upper, and set to work repairing this historical home. He also began advocating for historic preservation and equitable development in River Street. Bertram recalls the strong desire River Street residents had to improve their neighborhood. A large segment of the population continued pushing against urban renewal plans that would see their homes reduced to rubble. They also joined together to push for the creation of the Greenbelt as a recreation area and worked to create a community center. Both of these goals were realized during the 1970s.

River Street residents found themselves in a multi-ethnic community that was forged through discrimination. But, they were able to develop a community that looked beyond color and ethnicity.

Figure 38. St. Paul Baptist Church parsonage in 1950 (courtesy of the Idaho State Historical Archive).

Church and the River Street Community

Religion was central to the folks that lived in the River Street Neighborhood. Some long-time River Street residents have remarked that a church used to exist within the neighborhood at the corner of 14th Street and River but they could not recall what it was called. The name of this church and related information remains unknown and could not be identified at the Idaho State Archives.

Generally, River Street residents attended church outside the neighborhood. Boise's black community held church meetings in the back rooms of various businesses beginning in 1908. The best-known church attended by Boise's African Americans is St. Paul Baptist Church. In 1921, Rev. William Riley Hardy and members of the black community bought property outside the neighborhood at 124–128 Broadway Ave. and built a small church building and parish house. St. Paul remained at this address until 1998 when the building was moved to Julia Davis Park where it now serves as the Idaho Black History Museum.

River Street residents also fondly remember attending church functions at Bethel A.M.E. Church, among other Boise churches. The date in which Bethel was built could not be identified, but there are two photographs of parishioners from the 1930s and 1940.

Figure 39. St. Paul Baptist Church in its original location at 128 Broadway Ave., n.d. (courtesy of the Idaho State Historical Archive).

Below is a bibliography of newspaper articles related to St. Paul Baptist Church (view them at www.riverstreethistory.com):

Curfman, Eryn
2002 "Wall woes may force church to move." Idaho Statesman, 1/12/2002.
Statesman_2002_Church_May_Move

Stringfellow, Rosalie
1950 "Keys to St. Paul's Church Parsonage Presented to Pastor." Idaho Daily Statesman, 3/28/1850.
Statesman_1950_St_Pauls_Parsonage

Whaley, Susan
2002 "Faith of a Congregation." Idaho Statesman, 2/3/2002: 1,7.
Statesman_2002_Faith_of_congregation1

Wynn, Pat
1973 "The Role of St. Paul's Church as Cultural, Spiritual Center." Idaho Statesman 1/28/1973:4E.
Statesman_1973_St_paul_cultural_Center

Figure 40. St. Paul Baptist Church is now the Idaho Black History Museum, 2014 (White).

Figure 41. Bethel AME congregation, c.1935 (courtesy of the Idaho State Historical Archive).

Figure 42. Bethel AME choir, c.1940 (Ibid.).

Figure 43. Rev. Michael Ross ponders his church's future, 2002 (Ibid.).

Figure 44. Rev. Henry and Dr. Mamie Oliver in front of St. Paul Baptist Church, 1973 (Ibid.).

Figure 45. 1319 W. River Street is reported as once being a church in River Street (White 2014).

The Evolution of River Street

Historical maps provide another perspective of the neighborhood's evolution. The true story of the River Street Neighborhood is only told when combined with oral history interviews and archival documents. Boise, Idaho has been growing since the nineteenth century. Located along the Boise Riverbank, the River Street Neighborhood's growth has always been constrained by the river. Boise history changed with the channelization of the Boise River, but River Street was not completely developed until the 1970s. This video depicts the evolution of the neighborhood as seen through historical maps collected from the Idaho State Historical Society Archives in Boise.

> Visit www.riverstreethistory.com to see a video illustrating how the neighborhood changed throughout time.

Historical Maps Illustrate River Street's Development

Historical maps obtained from the Idaho State Historical Society show the evolution of the River Street Neighborhood. Although the Boise

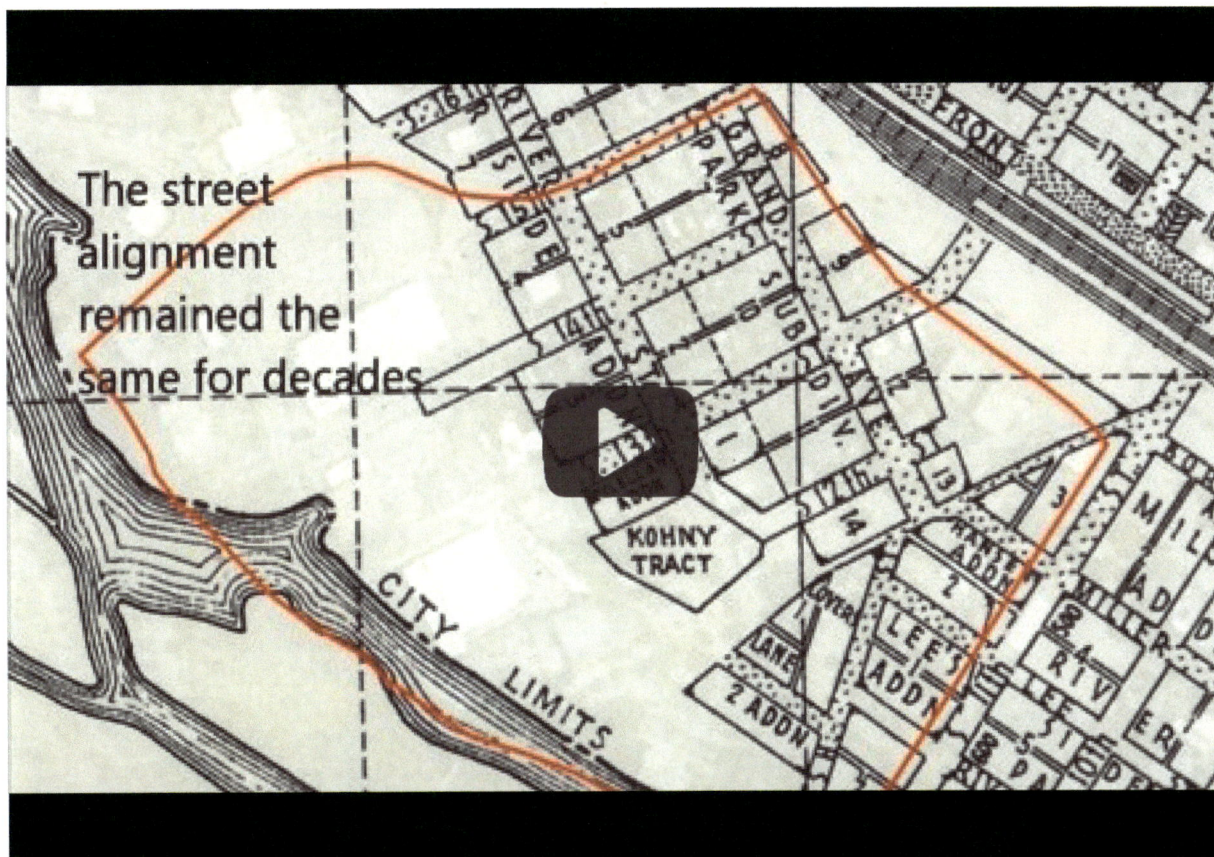

Figure 46. Still from video depicting the evolution of the River Street Neighborhood as shown on historical maps.

River was constrained early in the twentieth century, development along the riverbank did not occur until the 1970s. The City has always had a strong desire to see this place grow.

The initial platting of the River Street Neighborhood occurred during the late nineteenth century, in anticipation of the arrival of the Oregon Short Line Railroad. Prior to that, the area that would become the neighborhood was part of a number of land patents including that of John McClellan who platted the Riverside Addition in 1890.

McClellan's Riverside Addition led the way for additional plats, including Miller's Addition (1890) and the City Park Addition (1890s). The River Street Neighborhood was ready for development by 1900.

In 1891, the Boise River dominated River Street. The Riverside, City Park, and Miller's Additions are all part of River Street. The neighborhood is little more than a sketch at this time (Figure 47).

In the early 1900s, River Street residents had access to Riverside Park (Figure 48). The construction of Diversion Dam (1909) narrowed the Boise River, providing room for the Neighborhood to expand (Figure 49). There was room, but development of the floodplain was slow (Figure 50). The street alignments in River Street remained the same during the 1930s (Figure 51).

The 1964 City Map shows the Neighborhood just before major road realignments changed it forever. This shows the River Street Neighborhood prior to the street realignments that changed the community during the 1970s-1990s. In 1985,

Figure 47. 1891 City Map
Figure 48. 1907 City Map
Figure 49. 1917 City Map
Figure 50. 1935 City Map
Figure 51. 1941 City Map
Figure 52. 1964 City Map
(all, courtesy of the Idaho State Historical Archive).

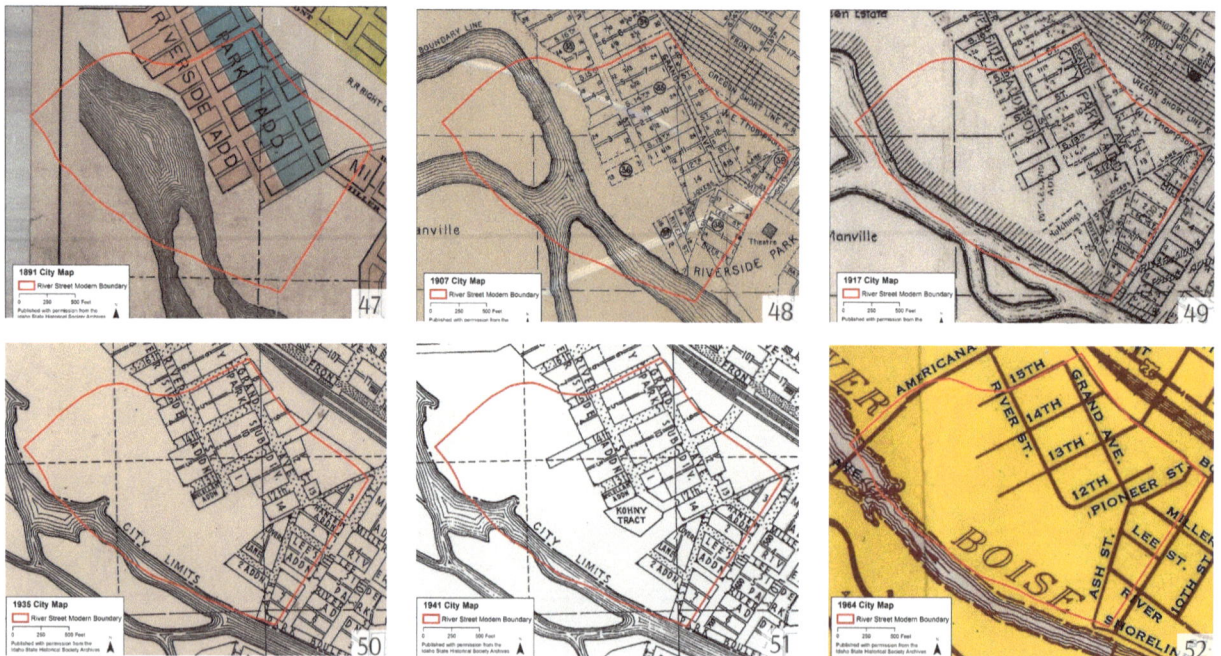

River Street was zoned for industrial development (Figure 52).

River Street in the Scope of Boise's Growth

The River Street Neighborhood is only a small portion of Boise, Idaho. Generous permissions granted by the Idaho State Historical Society Archives has allowed the collection of a range of Historical Boise, Idaho maps that show the overall growth of the town.

(NOTE: The digital files for these maps had to be shrunk in order to upload them to this website. You can contact the archives if you would like full-size, high-quality scans of these maps).

As is the story with all cities, the evolution of Boise and the River Street Neighborhood is documented in the historical maps that chronicle this change. River Street has been characterized by the location of the Boise River and the development whims of the Boise City government. Despite the fact that this place has been slated for industrial development, River Street remained home to hundreds of Boiseans since the 1890s.

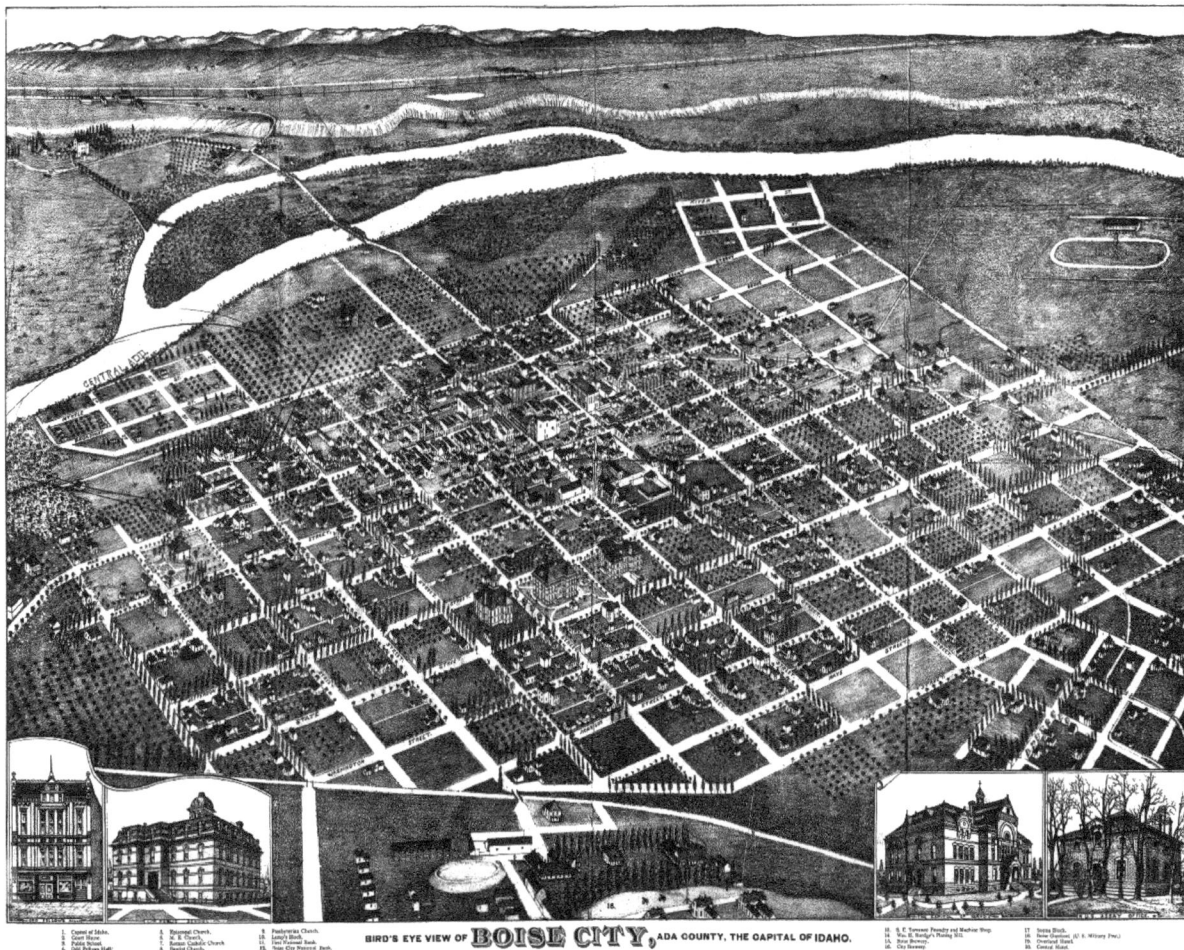

Figure 53. (left) One of the earliest maps depicting the River Street Neighborhood as an orchard by the river, 1887 (courtesy of the Idaho State Historical Archive).

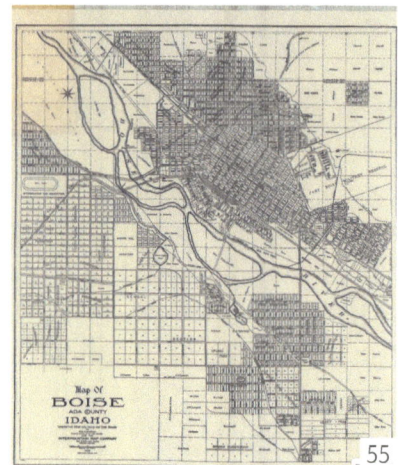

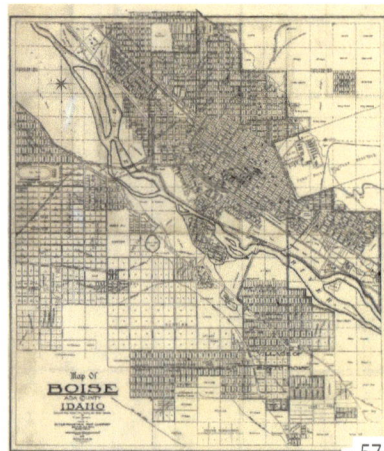

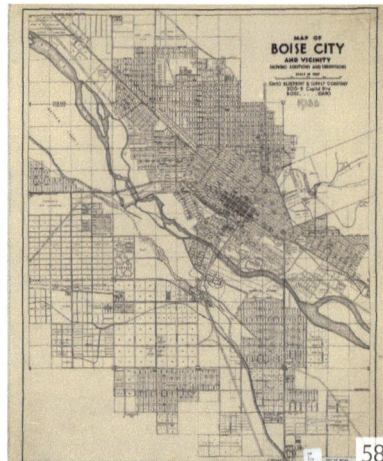

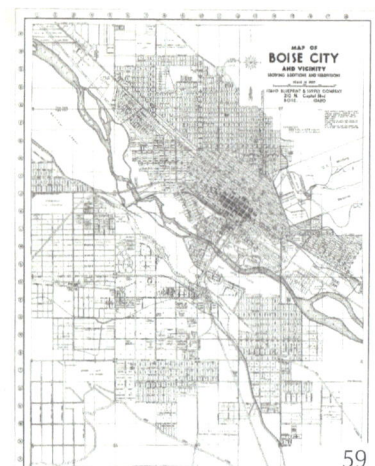

Figure 54. 1907 City Map, Riverside Park is a major attraction for the River Street Area (Ibid.).

Figure 55. 1909 City Map, the dynamic Boise River would be tamed by 1909 (Ibid.).

Figure 56. 1912 City Map, River Street remains nestled by the railroad tracks; Boise has expanded to the south far from the river (Ibid.).

Figure 57. 1917 City Map, River Street remains much as it was when originally platted nearly 20 years previously (Ibid.).

Figure 58. 1935 City Map, Julia Davis Park has been completed, but the floodplain near River Street remains undeveloped (courtesy of the Idaho State Historical Archive).

Figure 59. 1941 City Map, urban infill is increasing south of the Boise River by the 1940s (Ibid.).

An Assemblage of References Gleaned from Voluminous Stacks

Despite the fact that River Street has been a neighborhood for over 120 years, I found relatively few newspaper articles devoted to the neighborhood's people and history. Most of the documents I did find were on file at the Idaho State Historical Society Archives in Boise. You can download the latest newspaper article bibliography at www.riverstreethistory.com.

Tales told about the Neighborhood through Boise Newspapers

Most of the coverage about River Street comes from Boise's largest newspaper: the *Idaho Statesman*. While there is little on the community before the 1960s, most *Statesman* coverage vacillated between apathy about the "dying" community and frustration about how the city could effectively promote development. Statesman writer Tom Grote expressed the newspaper's coverage best in 1981 when he wrote:

> "Like parents of an errant child, Boise city officials and developers have been asking themselves: What shall we do about River Street?"

During the mid-twentieth century, the City of Boise was dedicated to transforming the Neighborhood in accordance with the prevailing tenets of Urban Renewal that was widespread throughout United States urban planning at the time. The idea was to create a regulatory framework that would encourage businesses to construct commercial properties in River Street. By the 1970s, the local news media appears to have been largely sold on the idea that River Street was decayed and dying—a blighted community. However, River Street residents would not be re-zoned or redeveloped out of their homes. In 1970, social work students at Boise State University and community activists were able to create a community center and playground. These amenities exist today. While residents fought for their neighborhood, other Boiseans regarded the place as a lost cause by the 1980s.

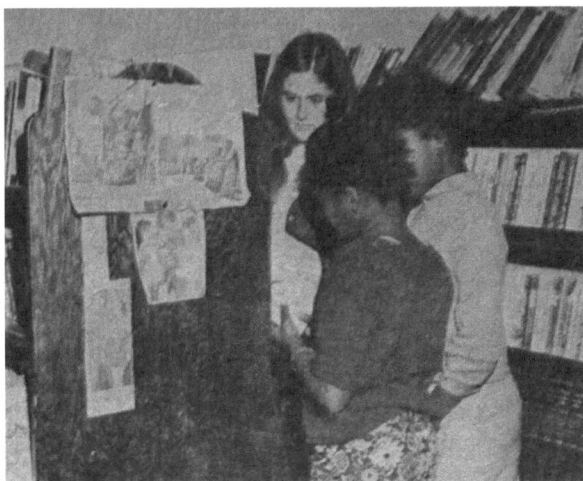

Figure 60. Youth at the River Street Community Center, 1970 (courtesy of the Idaho State Historical Archive).

By the early 2000s, the tune in Boise seems to have changed. *The Statesman* and *Boise Weekly* began reminiscing about the history that was being lost. River Street may be almost entirely lost, but its importance and heritage is slowly being acknowledged.

Below is a bibliography of newspaper articles related to the River Street Neighborhood that can be viewed at www.riverstreethistory.com:

Beebe, Paul
1987 "Developer says work to start on new offices." Idaho Statesman 6/3/1987. Statesman_6_3_1987_work_Started_on_Offices

Cameron, Mindy
1971 "Renewal Asked on River Street at Boise Parlay." Idaho Daily Statesman 10/8/1971:C6–7. Daily_Statesman_10-8-1971_Renewal_Asked_on_River_Street
1970 "River Street Center: A Successful Experiment." Idaho Statesman 12/13/1970:2E. Statesman_12-13-1970_River_Street_Center

Etlinger, Charles
1987 "Black Roots Go Deep in Idaho." Idaho Statesman 2/16/1987:1

Statesman_2-16-1987_Black_Roots_Go_Deep_in_Idaho

Ewing, Carrie
1970 "Owner Donates River Street Lot; Volunteers Map Playground Plan." Idaho Statesman 8/17/1970:10. Statesman_8-17-1981_Owner_Donates_River_Street_Lot

Friend, Janin
1986 "Office Complex Planned Along the River." Idaho Statesman 3/29/1986. Statesman_3_29_1986_OfficeComplex_Planned_on_river

Grote, Tom
1981 "River Street Poses Dilemma." Idaho Statesman 7/13/1981:1A. Statesman_7-13-1981_River_Street_Poses_Dilemma

Idaho Statesman
1981 "Once-thriving neighborhood exists in history alone." 3/25/1981. Statesman_3-25-1981_Once_Thriving_Neighborhood_Lives_in_Oral_History
1981 "River Street, Historic Preservation." 7/21/1981. Statesman_4_21_1981_River_Street_Historic_Preservation

Odoshi, Denise
2005 "Boise's Lee Street area now mostly a memory." Idaho Statesman 1/26/2005:1. Statesman_1-26-2005_Lee_Street_Mostly_a_Memory

Pewitt, Jana
1990 "Forest River IX will join complex by the Greenbelt." Idaho Statesman 7/25/1990. Statesman_7_25_1990_Forest_River_Complex

Winn, Christian A.
2001 "Down by the River: The Past, Present, and Future of a Historic Boise Neighborhood." Boise Weekly, Nov. 28–Dec.4. Boise_Weekly_11-28--12-4-2001_Down_by_the_River

Wyatt, Liz
2000 "River Street Neighborhood shows signs of renaissance." Idaho Statesman 6/11/2000: 1A,6A–7A. Statesman_6-11-2000_River_Street_Revival

Zarkin, David
1968 "Once-Proud River Street Area Hosted Boise's Cultural, Sporting Activities." Idaho Daily Statesman, 3/11/1968:14. Statesman_3-11-1968_River_Street_Hosted_Cultural_Activities

1968 "Variety of Zoning in Vicinity of Boise River Street Complicates Maintaining Standards in Residences." Idaho Daily Statesman, 3-12-68:pg. 5–C1. Daily_Statesman_3-12-1968_Zoning_in_River_Street_Complicates_Maintaining_Standards

Archival Oral History Transcripts

```
PROJECT SUMMARY

SURVEY OF LEE STREET NEIGHBORHOOD

     by Mateo Osa, Grantee
   Idaho Oral History Center
```

"In 1928, the city rezoned River Street unrestricted "F" zone. The original residential neighborhood remained intact while industrial and commercial growth took place on all sides which further isolated the area. It wasn't long before residents began to find the area less desirable and relocated in other growing areas of Boise." Mateo Osa, Survey of the Lee Street Neighborhood (1983)

In 1982, Mateo Osa recorded groundbreaking interviews with River Street's then aging African American population. This oral history project was the first of its kind in the River Street Neighborhood, which was then identified as "the Black Neighborhood." Osa proclaims that his project had the intent of gathering information about the Black settlement patterns on Lee Street, one of the most intact portions of the River Street Neighborhood today. In the process, Osa revealed much about the African American experience in Boise, Idaho. Transcripts of these interviews are on file at the Idaho State Archives in Boise.

```
NAME:   STEWART, Bessie
DATE:   December 17, 1980
INTERVIEWER:  Mateo Osa
LOCATION:  Boise, Idaho
```

"Yeah, that's right, World War II. There was a lot of servicemen because with the two bases at Gowen Field and Mountain Home. Well they were allowed to bring their wives and children who a few of them had children. And they just lived in every little hole they could. It was as I say, a lot of people made their garages into a little dwelling. At that time. But, then, it wasn't too long before the war was over and people left." Bessie Stewart's interview with Mateo Osa (12/17/1980).

Born into a tobacco farming family from Tennessee, Bessie Stewart moved to the Boise area in 1943 with her husband. She was able to convince her husband to purchase a home in the River Street Neighborhood during World War II and the couple promptly rented it out to African American servicemen and their families. A River Street resident for over 40 years, Mrs. Stewart recalled occasional discrimination in stores and businesses throughout Boise. She also had several remarks on the infamous Red Light District that existed along Pioneer Street/ Lover's Lane (the Pioneer Walkway today) during the 1940s and 1950s.

```
NAME:   THOMAS, Doris
DATE:   January 6, 1981
LOCATION:  1114 Lee Street
INTERVIEWER:  Mateo Osa
```

"I've raised all my kids down here and every one of them are good kids—they've all got good, responsible jobs and all have gone to college and everything, but there is some from over, oh, through Thirteenth, Fourteenth, Fifteenth, over through there, is where vandalism came from—not from our neighborhood.

This has always been a nice, quiet, respectable neighborhood." Doris Thomas' interview with Mateo Osa (1/6/1981).

Doris Thomas moved to Boise in 1926 and recalls that, despite its reputation, the River Street Neighborhood was composed of families from a variety of races and ethnicities. Basque immigrants and Chinese merchants found homes and livelihoods in there. The place was characterized by neighborliness—new families were helped by the existing residents. The neighborhood telephone was shared. People worked hard but shared what they had. *That's the way it was, just average middle-class, was what it was. It wasn't a slum area at all. Everybody kept their places up nice,"* Doris Thomas (1981).

```
NAME:   BUCKNER, DOROTHY
DATE:   January 23, 1981
LOCATION:  Boise, Idaho
INTERVIEWER:  Mateo Osa
SUBJECT:  Lee Street
REEL NO.:  375
OH NO.:  562
```

"Okay people, well my father hoboed to Idaho and then he'd send for the rest of the family and then I think he had a sister who's husband worked for the railroad, or something, and they could get a pass. They'd bring somebody else. That's the way people came." Dorothy Buckner's interview with Mateo Osa (1/23/1981).

Coming by way of Arkansas to Minidoka, Dorothy Buckner's family played an influential role in the black community of River Street. Her father, "Pistol" Johnson, operated a barbeque restaurant and repaired and rented houses in the Neighborhood for their absentee owners. She recalls that River Street was home to African American Boiseans not only because of the draw of community; discrimination kept African Americans there. Mrs. Buckner remembers when

Boise's African Americans joined the Civil Rights Movement and began pushing for their rights. Not everybody in the community thought that was a good idea, but Mrs. Buckner was not one to be kept down. After moving from the neighborhood, Mrs. Buckner recalls a cross burning in the front yard of her North End home. Not to be deterred, Buckner stayed in that home for over twenty years.

```
NAME:  PERKINS, Ellen Stevens
DATE:  December 16, 1980
INTERVIEWER:  Mateo Osa
LOCATION: Boise, Idaho
```

"I shall never forget when my husband died. The neighbors right straight across over there, came to me and said, 'We are not just your neighbors, we are your friends. If you need anything or want anything or anything comes up that you can't take care of, call us.' And they have proved to be my friends." Ellen Perkins' interview with Mateo Osa (12/16/1980).

Longtime fixture of the River Street Neighborhood, Ellen Perkins came from a family that owned several properties in the neighborhood. Her family was from Arkansas and, for a short while, she tried to reconnect with her ancestral home but ended up right back home in Boise. For her, life in River Street was characterized by kindness, sharing, and community. Through discrimination, Mrs. Perkins remembers neighborhood residents finding a way to live side by side.

```
INTERVIEWER:  Rosa Tigner
DATE:  February 6, 1981
LOCATION: Boise, Idaho
INTERVIEWER:  Mateo Osa
```

"Oh, in Pocatello we are freer with one another. Boise was rather reserved, I mean both the Blacks and Whites. We more or less, a newcommer or a johnny-come-lately had to prove themselves. But once you got over that, it's okay. But I'd rather live in Pocatello." Rosa Tigner's interview with Mateo Osa (2/6/1981).

Coming from Texas, Rosa Tigner grew up in Pocatello, Idaho and moved to the River Street Neighborhood with her husband. Mrs. Tigner recalls the way racial relations in the United States improved after World War II. With black and white men fighting in the trenches together, both came to understand that discrimination was not in this country's best interest. She recalls that conditions for African Americans were better in Idaho than Texas, but felt that the black community in Boise was standoffish. Newcomers had to prove themselves before they were accepted. Tigner believed the small Black community in River Street made it more conservative than comparatively more cosmopolitan Pocatello.

Interviews with some of the neighborhoods current and former residents revealed a community where persons of all races and creeds were judged based on the content of their character. In this place where Boise's "others" were permitted to live, River Street residents found a way to get along and interact against a backdrop of a less permissive society.

Visit www.riverstreethistory.com for highlights from some of River Street's former residents' reminiscences. The complete audio recordings of these interviews will be available for public use at the Idaho State Historical Society's Archives in Boise. Also find oral histories completed in 2014 with Dick Madry, John Bertram, Lee Rice, II, and Warner Terrell, III.

(Interviews and tags courtesy of the Idaho State Historical Archive). Interview transcripts can be found at www.riverstreethistory.com.

2014 Oral History Interviews

In the summer of 2014, oral history interviews were recorded with four former residents of the River Street Neighborhood. The interview with Warner Terrell, III and Dick Madry was conducted at the Idaho Black History Museum in Boise on June 16. Later that day, another interview was recorded with John Bertram at his office in River Street. The interview with Lee Rice, II was recorded on June 18, 2014 at his office off Vista Avenue. All of these interviews concentrated on revealing the racial dynamics that existed between neighborhood residents and the rest of the community. All four of these men grew up in River Street and recall how the neighborhood used to be.

Life on "the Hang": John Bertram's life in River Street

The child of a college professor, John Bertram moved up and down the Pacific Coast during his youth. He was a college student at the University of Washington in 1968 when he was drafted to the Vietnam War. Bertram ended up joining VISTA (Volunteers in Service to America), a branch of the AmeriCorps program. He was trained in New York and was sent to Idaho for service. With an interest in urban planning, Bertram asked to be placed in the largest city in Idaho. He found himself living in a house on Lee Street in the River Street Neighborhood

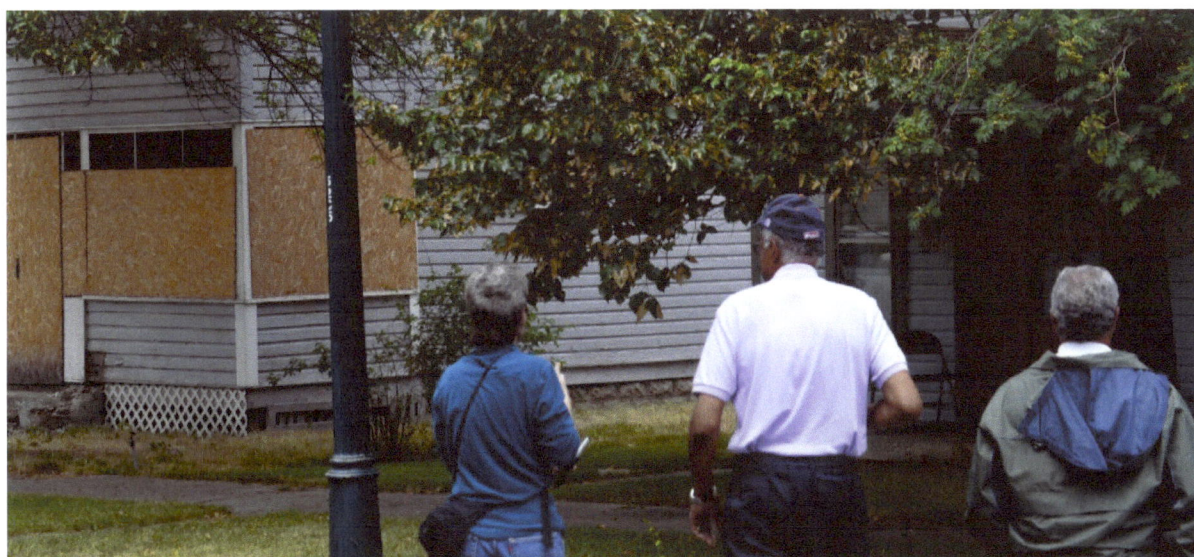

Figure 61. (bottom) From left to right: Dr. Jill Gill, Warner Terrell, III, and Dick Madry during a neighborhood site visit, 2014 (White).

living next to Rosa Tigner.

> **"[19]'69 was still a time when River Street still was kind of the other side of the tracks. It had a fairly predominant African American population...There was a pretty large white community here during that same time"** (Bertram 2014).

Working in River Street, Bertram was involved in a lot of programs. He worked with the food stamp program in Boise (Al Ada Community Action Network) and helped demonstrate the poverty that existed in Boise. He helped found a park in the neighborhood as well. Working with a student group at Boise State University, he helped paint a number of houses in the neighborhood. His job was to serve those in need.

> **"Boise is a good community. If you ask for a paintbrush and a bucket of paint for a good cause, people will give it to you"** (Bertram 2014).

He worked on several development plans for the neighborhood that focused on building more and improving existing residential housing. His plan involved accentuating the residential aspect of the neighborhood, but commercial development interests were frequently at odds with Bertram's plans. He recognizes that "you didn't need a car to live here" (River Street) because there were stores and other amenities that made the neighborhood walkable. Unfortunately, commercial properties were built along the riverfront, essentially cutting River Street off from the Boise River and eliminating of the free space the neighborhood used to enjoy. Some of his plans did become a reality. The River Street community donated some of its redevelopment funding to help construct the Greenbelt and a community park was built during Bertram's residency here. His advocacy also helped turn the 8th Street Marketplace into a historical commercial development, save the 8th Street Bridge, and erect new residential buildings in the neighborhood.

The demise of local grocery stores such as Zurcher's and Pearl Grocery came around the time Bertram arrived to the neighborhood. During the 1960s, large stores like Smith's Food King and K-mart spelled the end of small local stores.

Figure 62. Men work on a house in River Street, 1970 (from the collection of John Bertram).

Figure 63. Pearl Grocery serviced the neighborhood until the late 1960s (courtesy of the Idaho State Historical Archive).

Bertram recalls, during the early twentieth century skilled professionals and tradespeople used to live in the neighborhood. The grandfather of Charles Hummel, one of the architects that designed the Idaho State Capitol, lived in the River Street Neighborhood on 13th Street. It is likely that these professionals moved away when the neighborhood was zoned for industrial development..

Bertram came back to River Street when his VISTA service was over. He worked for the 8th Street Marketplace for a few years and bought a house in the neighborhood. Bertram moved in and began improving the house over the next few years. He raised a family and kept the River Street house as a rental.

Living in River Street was living life in "the Hang". "The Hang" was the community that made African Americans feel welcome in the River Street Neighborhood. Bertram recalls that black Job Corps kids and military soldiers used to come to the neighborhood and just hang out because they felt more comfortable there than in the rest of the city. He believes that, today, the entire town is open to blacks in a way that used to not exist.

> **"What was really lovely about the neighborhood was most of my neighbors were African American and they were closer to me than most of my current neighborhood neighbors that I live with. Again, we didn't have Thanksgiving together, but there was a rapport and there was a trust..." (Bertram 2014).**

The troublesome thing about River Street today is that a lot of this camaraderie has been lost. He believes that a good neighborhood is composed of people of all different races, ethnicities, and classes. However, other residents do not feel that way. Currently, there is a homeless shelter in River Street and Bertram laments the fact that property owners are walling their properties off because they do not feel comfortable with the presence of homeless people. He feels like these walls literally cut people off from the folks living around them, which stymies the dynamic sense of belonging and cooperation that characterized the neighborhood when he first moved there.

Grandma's House: Dick Madry and Childhood in the Neighborhood

Dick Madry's great grandparents came to Idaho from Missouri sometime in the 1890s. Lured to Nampa to do railroad work, Madry's great grandparents had 13 children and initially lived in a farmstead near Nampa. He was raised by his grandmother, Erma Hayman, who moved to Boise in the 1930s, bought a house in 1947, and lived there until 2009.

River Street was known for its illicit activity, but many former residents have been reluctant to acknowledge this. While it was not a positive part of life in the neighborhood, Madry remembered the goings on in those "joints". He remembered "Pistol" Johnson's entrepreneurial ventures including Blackjack's Barbeque, operating as an informal pawnbroker, and several other underground activities. Despite these illicit ventures, Johnson played an important role in the neighborhood by providing money to those that needed it. Recalling the gambling and prostitution houses along Pioneer Street (the Pioneer Walkway), Madry had the following to say:

> **"It wasn't just after hours either. There were several along what is now the Pioneer Street corridor...There were some on South 13th that I remember."**

Before these houses became Joints, they were regular residential houses. Madry recalls hearing from his grandmother that Senator William Borah used to visit the Pioneer Street area in order to connect with his working class constituents. Madry had several relatives that used to live in that area before it was vilified by the houses of ill-repute.

As a child, Madry always had chores and home-work. He typically had to haul wood or coal and water or mow the yard upon returning home from school. He also took care of the garden, pulling weeds and watering the vegetables. Each family in River Street grew their own garden in the yard of their house. Madry remembers that it didn't matter what race you were or whether or not you owned or rented your home, almost everybody in River Street had a garden. In addition to the garden, Madry's family also had fruit trees: peaches, cherries, and apples that were also canned for later consumption. They also kept chickens.

People in the neighborhood did things together and racial lines were crossed in the neighbor-hood, according to Madry. Both black and white cooperated and worked together to make their community a better place to live. Madry remembers that, in the neighborhood, people of all races got along well and there was little discrimination between residents. He remem-bers River Street being a safe place where a family could raise their children without having to worry about overt racial discrimination. This contrasted with the rest of the town, especially "upstanding" citizens that did everything they could to avoid River Street. Madry explained that discrimination came from outside the neighborhood. While it was not like conditions in the Deep South, River Street residents were more likely to experience discrimination out-side the neighborhood than inside it.

Playing down by the River: Lee Rice, II and Childhood in the Neighborhood

Growing up in River Street during the 1960s and 1970s, Lee Rice, II recalls it as a diverse com-munity. Interpersonal relationships were based on familiarity rather than race and even people from outside the neighborhood were welcome.

Figure 64. Dick Madry's grandmother's house is one of the few historical homes left in River Street, 2014 (White).

"Even my friends from school would come over and hang out at the house, come over to the neighborhood...In high school when everything else was closed down there was always something happening. There was always some sort of house party." (Rice 2014).

Everyone from the neighborhood had an understanding of what it was like to live in the neighborhood, but because there were so few blacks in Boise, most people from the town knew who the black kids were and knew their families. Euroamericans in the rest of the city wanted African Americans to live in River Street, but, because they had years of contact with the neighborhood's black people, the overt attempts at discrimination were lessened. Rice recalls some discrimination, but was not brought up that way. His family did not discriminate and based relationships on an individual's character. However, the negative identity of the neighborhood provided protection. Whites were reluctant to enter the neighborhood, so folks living "South of the Tracks" were safe in the neighborhood.

Rice recalls what happened to African Americans who decided to move outside of River Street. The Buckner family was among the first blacks to move from River Street to another part of town—the now historic North End district. African Americans in Boise recall that, in an attempt to scare the Buckner family back into the neighborhood, white Boiseans burned a cross in their front yard. The tactic did not work and members of the Buckner family still live in the North End. Rice recalls that the cross burning was an eye-opening event for River Street's black community. Many of them were shocked to hear that such a thing happened, but the event proved the lengths Euroamericans in Boise would go in order to maintain segregation.

Kids from River Street used to play along the river. Rice recalls hanging onto a small rope bridge to cross the river and play on the other side:

"We used to swim across the river to go to the park...Just at the Americana Bridge...you would cross there. And these rocks, they were jagged, the water's rushing and they had this wire. And we would navigate across that and it was no problem...Sometimes we might slip and fall but it wasn't anything major." (Rice 2014).

He laments the fact that, today, children are not given this opportunity. Rice stated that if the same thing were to happen today, the police would most likely get involved and stop the whole thing. In the past, that was simply how children played.

River Street children were like millions of other young Americans. They had chores such as watering the yard and tending to the garden. Kids in the neighborhood played ball in the street. Hours of fun were had at the gravel pit that occupied a portion of a currently paved parking lot. The Boise River was also a favorite playing area and lagoons that existed before the Greenbelt was created were attractions for the neighborhood children.

Lee Rice has big plans for the neighborhood. He has long hoped for River Street to have additional commercial venues to be added and foresees several other development projects in the area. Rice would like to see existing commercial buildings house businesses that would serve the community and for vacant lots to be developed into housing or additional commercial venues. He has not given up hope on his former home.

Most importantly, Rice wants the world to know that River Street was much more than

Figure 65. Bernease and Arthir Rice, n.d. (from the collection of Lee Rice, II).

Figure 66. Arthur Rice and his wife Bernease raised their kids in River Street, n.d. (Ibid.)

Figure 67. River Street resident Bernease Rice, n.d. (Ibid.).

Figure 68. The Shines family before they emigrated to River Street in the mid-twentieth century, n.d. (Ibid.).

Figure 69. Bernease Rice and her son Lee, II in River Street, c.1950 (Ibid.).

"the Black Neighborhood". It was a place where familiarity and community were the rule. People in the neighborhood got along and overlooked race lines in order to forge a community where kids could play safely and grow into productive adults.

Mr. Rice was extremely generous and provided several historical photographs related to his family's tenure in the River Street Neighborhood.

Class President, Gardener, and Hunter: Warner Terrell, III talks about Growing up in River Street

The first of the Terrell Family members arrived to River Street over 100 years ago. Coming from North Carolina, Warner Terrell, III's grandfather came to Boise in 1905 with his half-brother to work on the railroad. In 1905, Terrell, III's grandfather bought a house in River Street at 527 South 14th Street and brought the rest of his family up from Utah. Terrell, III's father, Warner Tarrell, Jr was born and ultimately married in that house on S. 14th Street. Warner Terrell, III had one sister, Zenobia, and a half brother, James. Terrell's mother (Clara Terrell) was born in Rigby, Idaho and was a member of the African American Steven's family.

Both of Terrell, III's parents worked: his mother as a housekeeper and his father at the Arid Club for over 45 years. The Terrells served as point people for new black arrivals to town, helping them find housing and work after arriving to Boise.

Terrell, III recalled a few memorable discriminatory acts that served to keep blacks in their place. For instance, when famed African American singer Marian Anderson came to Boise she was refused lodging at the Owyhee Hotel—one of the town's premier hotels at the time. She was later allowed to stay at the Owyhee as long as she agreed to enter through the back entrance and take her food in her hotel room. Marian Anderson was one of the most famous black singers of the twentieth century, breaking the color barrier for other black artists. She gave a critically acclaimed concert at the Lincoln Memorial in 1939 and was the first African American to perform at the Metropolitan Opera in New York City. Nevertheless, the Owyhee Hotel in Boise, Idaho initially refused her service. Warner Terrell, III's father helped arrange Anderson's lodging at the Owyhee Hotel. Terrell did note that conditions had changed by the second time she came.

He also talked about the underground activities along Pioneer Street. Several players helped make the red light district possible. For instance, a colorful neighborhood fixture called "Big Mama" operated some brothels in the neighborhood, and Terrell, III recalls that she was a nice lady that regularly attended Bethel AME Methodist Church. She was generous to all and maintained good relations with the Boise City Police.

"If you drove through Pioneer Street, there would be a whole line up. Waiting to get in the houses."

The red light district on Pioneer was frequented by all types of people ranging in age from teenagers to older professional men. Terrell, III explains that the district was created slowly over time. At first, one or two rental houses turned into gambling spots or brothels but, over time, their number increased. As long as the owners were getting their rent, many of them did not care what was happening in their properties. Eventually, the whole street had turned into a red light district and the other residents just avoided those places.

Figure 70. Terrell children riding bikes in River Street, n.d. (courtesy of the Idaho State Historical Archive).

"That was there and one probably started and those people kinda hung together. And then the rest of the people just avoided them."

Terrell, III recalls being told to avoid Pioneer and he listened to his parents. He never played near the Joints, staying near his home or the houses of his other relatives. In addition to houses of ill repute, the neighborhood also suffered from industrial pollution. Positioned by the railroad tracks and an industrial district, River Street could be a gritty place. Terrell, III recalls trains passing by, spewing smoke on the houses that flanked the south side of the track.

After school, time was spent in a similar fashion as other River Street kids. Terrell, III had chores after school including tending the garden, watering the lawn, and helping tidy the house. In the summer, he recalls helping till the soil in his back yard in order to plant a garden with his grandmother. "It was her garden, but I think I did most of the work," Terrell, III recalls. Gardens in the neighborhood contained a variety of different vegetables that were primarily eaten by the family. What wasn't eaten fresh was canned for later consumption. River Street residents also did other activities to help make ends meet. For instance, Terrell, III's grandfather used to chop and sell kindling and collected honey when sugar was rationed during World War II.

Figure 71. One of the Terrell family children with a goat and cart, n.d. (courtesy of the Idaho State Historical Archive).

Outdoor recreation was also important to River Street residents. Terrell, III recalls doing a lot of hunting and fishing with his relatives. He fished in the Boise River for a variety of species, catfish, trout, steelhead, and salmon. He mainly hunted birds on agricultural fields near present-day Eagle, Idaho.

While there was discrimination in Boise, Terrell recalls that his fellow students were amiable and cordial. He was student body president at North Junior High and does not recall having trouble finding dates in high school. Schools were integrated and interracial dating was okay in the neighborhood, but Euroamericans from outside the neighborhood frowned on interracial dating. Terrell recalls an instance when he was talking to a friend from school, a white girl, when a Boise Police officer drove by and saw them talking. The white police officer stopped and forced the girl to get in the car. He took the girl to the police station and made her call her parents and tell them what she was doing.

Growing up in River Street, Terrell, III recalls a happy childhood in a community that shielded him from overt racist acts. He agrees that neighborliness was a way of life in River Street. Residents overcame many of the racial taboos of that time, including interracial dating; however, that was not the case elsewhere in Boise. His youth was filled with hunting and fishing—activities that he still enjoys today. He says the neighborhood has changed and the community he enjoyed as a youth no longer exists today.

Visit www.riverstreethistory.com to hear the memories of those interviewed in 2014.

How River Street Helped Create Whiteness in Boise, Idaho

An Anthropological Interpretation

River Street was integral to the creation of "whiteness" as a distinct racial identity in Boise. It may have been inhabited by multiple races and ethnicities, but the role of this neighborhood was to create a distinctly separate place where non-Euroamerican people could live without integrating into the rest of the city. Racial mores in the United States for most of the twentieth century forced Americans to live in a segregated society. Much of this was designed to maintain white privilege, but it also had the side effect of creating self-contained, close-knit ethnic communities. In Boise, River Street was occupied by whites, blacks, and other non-Euroamericans; however, it functioned as a container for the "others"—people that were not allowed to be considered part of Euroamerican Boise.

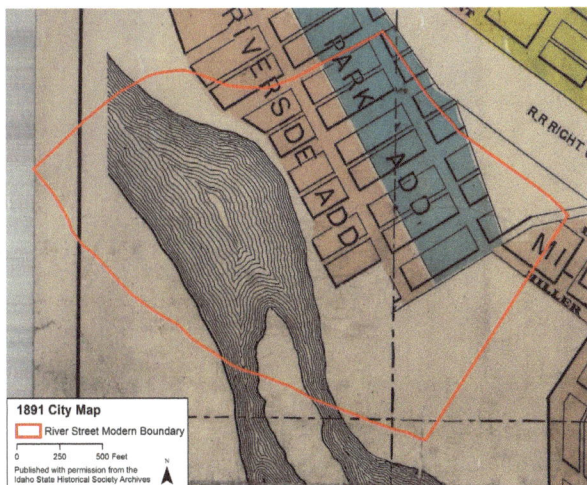

Figure 72. The current boundaries of the River Street Neighborhood overlain upon an 1891 Boise City Plat map (courtesy of the Idaho State Historical Archive).

My experience and education as an anthropologist gives me a unique perspective on this process. One of the most interesting aspects of this project is examining the way the River Street Neighborhood helped create whiteness in Boise.

Whiteness, Development, and Historic Preservation

City governments across the United States found reasons to embrace "urban renewal" during the mid-twentieth century. The roots of urban renewal can be found in the Housing Act of 1949, which provided an unprecedented public funds commitment to the physical and economic restructuring of American cities. During the 1950s and 1960s, as much as $10 billion in tax dollars were used to fund over 2,100 renewal projects. Renewal focused on "blighted" neighborhoods that, oftentimes, were occupied by non-Euroamericans—especially African Americans. The huge swaths of the urban landscape that were demolished to make way for new urban construction quickly caused a public uproar. Boise, Idaho was no different than hundreds of other towns in their zeal for removing blight with a wrecking ball. Renewal in Boise also focused on the town's only African American neighborhood (Demo 2006). By the 1970s, African Americans and preservation-minded, middle-class Americans had joined forces to stop the demolition (Reichl 1997).

While most of the blight in downtown Boise had been removed by this time, various development plans for the River Street Neighborhood made it contested ground. Residents fought for their homes. Planners sought to improve the city through new construction.

Urban renewal was as much about reconfiguring urban spaces as it was about reconfiguring the urban social fabric. Designed and executed by governments that were overwhelmingly Euroamerican, urban renewal focused on poor, non-White neighborhoods and prioritized the creation of a highway system that allowed an escape from urban life or the construction of central shopping malls while simultaneously destroying the fabric of non-White neighborhoods, forcing them to move elsewhere (Cashin 2008:57). This was certainly the case in Boise.

While other researchers have covered the effects of renewal (Fullilove 2009) and gentrification (Hyra 2008) on black neighborhoods in other parts of the country, little, if any investigation has been invested in studying the effect of this process on smaller black communities in the American West. The River Street Neighborhood became part of Boise's urban landscape between the 1890s and 1923 and was the site of a diverse, multi-ethnic community where African American, Basque, Euroamericans, and immigrants from other European nations were able to buy and rent homes (Demo 2006:13–18, 5–27). It was home to the folks from the "south side of the tracks"– the "others". This small enclave of minority groups composed an important social category that allowed the existence of Euroamericans because they were part of the "other", a hierarchical social designation that enabled the demarcation and social privilege of Euroamericans as a race.

Today, the River Street Neighborhood exists in the memory of its former residents, in documents curated by local archives, and on the landscape. Social dynamics caused by the racialization process between River Street Neighborhood residents and Euroamericans residing outside the neighborhood have already been revealed in existing stories and interpretations of the neighborhood (Demo 2006; Buckner 1981; Hayman 1980; Stewart 1980). Other aspects of racialization in Boise will undoubtedly be revealed in the future oral histories and historical archaeological work.

The Creation of Whiteness and Racial Privilege in Boise

The history of racialization in Boise is complex; however, the dialectic between African Americans and Euroamericans can fittingly be examined by positioning Boise within a larger, worldwide capitalist system. The status of social groups in hierarchical capitalist systems is situational and highly entangled. Anthropologists can only analyze social groups, including races, while also simultaneously considering neighboring groups in society because no social group lives and operates in isolation. Eric Wolf writes in the introduction to his landmark book *Europe and the People without History*, "...there can be no 'Black history' apart from 'White history', only a component of common history suppressed or omitted from conventional studies for economic, political, or ideological reasons." (1997:19).

Wolf understood the way social structures form networks that bind communities together in such a way that individual social groups cannot be easily separated from each other. In the United States, racial hierarchies serve to reinforce class affiliations that were intended to guarantee economic and social benefits for one particular race—Euroamericans. Researchers of whiteness as a racial ontology point out that while racial designations exist, race is actually lived in class-specific ways that can be seen in places like historical Boise, Idaho (Epperson 2004; Hartigan 1997:498; Mullins 1999). In the case of River Street, white Boiseans needed non-whites in order to establish themselves as a distinct social group. This distinction was created in part by the racialization process which uses real or perceived physiological characteristics to create social groups or subgroups. These differences are also used to place distinct social groups within the wider hierarchy that exists in that culture. The aim for whites is to place themselves in a privileged position in order to aggrandize power (Hartmann et al. 2009).

In order to understand the role that racialization has played out for Euroamericans, it is important to understand the role that racial identities have played in the historical, social, political, and economic landscape of the United States. Most importantly for the analysis of racial identities in River Street, anthropologists must remember that such identities are fluid and context specific. Racial identities are purely ideological concepts that are a means of separating human populations and are principally created by those who play a role in the formation of social hierarchies. Central to

the racialization process is the use of real or perceived physiological differences to strategically create a hierarchy in which some races are judged to be superior to others (Orser 2007, 2004:115–118). In the United States, this hierarchy has been structurally designed to define and maintain social relations between various racial groups, most prominently Euroamericans versus "the other"; and to control access to goods, political power, economic strength, and overall life opportunities (Hartmann et al. 2009; Orser 2007).

Whiteness, thus, is a state of mind, an ideological construct that becomes perpetuated through discourse, practice, and daily behaviors of which most people are unaware but nonetheless preserve racial identity (Hartmann et al. 2009). Ruth Frankenberg (1997:1) argues that "white studies" in the social sciences focus on three core theoretical positions and hypotheses: 1) whiteness is a location of structural advantage of race privilege; 2) it is a standpoint from which white people look at themselves, others, and society, and; 3) whiteness refers to a set of cultural practices that are usually unmarked and unnamed (Hartmann et al. 2009:406).

Figure 73. The arrival of the Oregon Short Line Railroad in the 1890s cleaved River Street from the rest of Boise's urban landscape (courtesy of the Idaho State Historical Archive).

The historical population of African Americans in Boise are descendants of African slaves brought to the United States; however, the racialization of both Euroamericans and African Americans is predicated upon racial mores developed during the period of American slavery (roughly 1619–1865). Following the abolition of slavery in the United States, African American identity continued to be plagued by negative connotations and were placed in a permanent working class status within the American social hierarchy. This proletariat status was a necessary element of American capitalist society that requires workers to perform all manner of tasks. White discrimination kept blacks in a proletariat caste and this social position was replicated in Boise's social and geographic landscape (Demo 2006).

Power differentials created through race and class differentiation are similar to descriptions of social power dialectics originally outlined by Marxist theorists in the social sciences. The Marxist dialectic is particularly useful in the case of River Street because it simplifies the interplay of two principal racial categories in historical Boise: Euroamericans, who strove to maintain social, economic, and moral control of the community, and the diverse array of social groups categorized by Euroamericans as the "others" who worked to dismantle their stigmatization. The "others" category specifically targeted African Americans but frequently included other non-Euroamericans and Euroamericans that were stigmatized because they lived alongside and interacted with the "others".

River Street as a Historical Landscape of Segregation

In Boise, the most visible material manifestation of racialization is the urban landscape of the River Street Neighborhood. While porous and constantly subject to change, the preeminence of Euroamerican identity had long been intact in American society by the time Boise was created and, certainly, by the time African Americans moved to River Street (Hartigan 2005; Jacobson 1998:31–38; Roediger 1991). The social construction of race generally entails the segregation of space along racial categories; subsequently, racially homogeneous groups construct their own places and develop a sense of place to fulfill social and cultural needs and obligations. In Boise, River Street served to reinforce racial segregation, which, in turn, served to maintain Euroamerican hegemony by creating a place of contrast—the geographic home of the others (Oliver 1990; White 2014).

This geographic segregation also played an important role in the economy of Boise, especially with regard to real estate values where racism played a significant role in the character and perceived value of property. Neighborhoods with African American and other non-Euroamerican residents were considered less desirable places to live and properties in these places were valued at a lower price. Euroamerican homeowners in the rest of Boise had a strong motivation to keep African Americans in a discrete geographic area in order to prevent the racist devaluation of their own homes due to the presence of African American neighbors (Demo 2006; Oliver 1990; Stewart 1980). The economic devaluation of houses in the neighborhood also made it easier to characterize this place as blighted and worthy of Urban Renewal and unworthy of historic preservation.

In addition to creating a place where African Americans could be "contained", Euroamerican real estate speculators were also creating a neighborhood dedicated to speculation. Archival documents explain that the area that became the River Street Neighborhood was once a farmstead that was sold to real estate speculators in advance of the arrival of the railroad. From the 1890s–1920s, these investors and a small number of private property owners built prefabricated, single-family houses with the intention of renting the dwellings out to working-class employees of the nearby railroad warehouses and in downtown Boise. The neighborhood's location south of the tracks geographically separated River Street from the rest of Boise and quickly became known for its African American residents who arrived as railroad employees (Demo 2006; Osa 1981). From its inception, River Street was considered a place for financial gain by developers and absentee property owners but, due to its geographic location and black residents, it also became a lynchpin in maintaining white hegemony in Boise.

Racial designations in the United States were an outgrowth of the global expansion of capitalism. The racialization process (i.e. exploiting divisions between different social groups based on physiological differentiations) was used and perpetuated in order to hierarchically place social groups within the greater society. In Boise, the social hierarchy was dedicated toward preserving Euroamerican preeminence which allowed this group to claim an inordinate proportion of political, social, and economic power; however, as evidenced in Wolf's introduction, the relationships between social groups and motivations for action are tightly entangled. Euroamerican real estate speculators intended on using River Street for financial gain, but they were also able to use the neighborhood to maintain social structures that gave them privileges because of their racial affiliation. The materiality of these activities is intrinsically linked to the manifestation and maintenance of a hierarchy of social groups. River Street and racialization in Boise can be viewed as a single case study in the complicated ways race-based hegemony played out in the United States.

Visit www.riverstreethistory.com to learn more about River Street as a landscape of memory or memoryscape.

Race and Class Struggles: A View from the River Street Neighborhood

Racial dynamics that led to the creation of the River Street Neighborhood also served to reinforce class divisions and ensure the position of Boise's Euroamerican elites. The neighborhood was created in anticipation of the 1893 arrival of the Oregon Short Line Railroad. Real estate speculators, who were all initially Euroamerican, quickly bought and subdivided parcels along the south side of the railroad tracks. The goal was to provide jobs and housing for the warehouse workers and other working class service industry employees in nearby downtown Boise. Sandwiched between the railroad, a warehouse/industrial strip and the Boise River, the neighborhood became a prime location to house Boise's "others". From the 1920s to the 1960s, River Street was primarily occupied by blacks, immigrants, and poor white families (Demo 2006).

African American newcomers were housed in River Street for a number of reasons. Idaho was a free territory and a free state meaning African Americans that came to the state could not be enslaved. Most African Americans that arrived in Boise before the 1920s were railroad workers or employed in various restaurants, hotels, and service industry businesses in downtown Boise. The proximity of River Street to railroad warehouses, railroad-related businesses, and downtown made it a prime location to house this new demographic. Additionally, the River Street neighborhood remained newly platted and not completely infilled when African Americans began to arrive. Undeveloped lots remained until the 1920s. The geographic segregation of the neighborhood from downtown and the rest of Boise made it an excellent place for segregation. As non-Euroamericans arrived to town during the early twentieth century, they were forced to live in River Street due to segregation (Demo 2006).

Boise's Euroamericans went to great measures to keep River Street as the home of the "others". African Americans were the primary target of their discrimination, but poor whites were oftentimes negatively affected by racialization efforts. Euroamerican elites enlisted intellectuals in the local government and business groups to maintain real estate and economic sanctions that prevented blacks from renting or buying houses outside the neighborhood and unevenly taxed their businesses (Demo 2006; Stewart 1980).

Territorial Stigmatization for River Street's White Residents

The quest to maintain white hegemony in Boise sometimes affected other whites. Poor white residents of River Street were stigmatized because of where they lived and were, thus, bypassed by job promotions and other economic opportunities. This process, which also effected African Americans, has been called "territorial stigmatization" by Loïs Wacquant. Territorial stigmatization creates a social and economic, self-fulfilling prophesy where residents of places like River Street have decreased opportunities because of the negative connotations associated with being residents of a neighborhood with a bad reputation. Describing the way territorial stigmatization is reinforced by the surrounding community, Wacquant (2010:218) explains:

> "...on the external front, spatial stigma alters the perception and skews the judgments and actions of the surrounding citizenry, commercial operators, and government officials. Outsiders fear coming into the neighborhood and commonly impute a wide range of

nefarious traits to its inhabitants. Businesses are reticent to open facilities or to provide services for customers in 'no-go areas." Employers hesitate to hire job applicants who, coming from them, are unreflectively suspected of having a lax work ethic and lower moral standards, leading to pervasive 'address discrimination.'"

In the case of River Street, both white and black residents found themselves stigmatized because of where they lived, even though Euroamerican River Street residents were phenotypically members of the race that benefitted most from hegemony. Both blacks and white neighborhood residents were limited to low-wage work and homes that were perceived as lower quality housing; however, former residents are quick to note that owner-occupied houses were a symbol of pride and better maintained than rentals (Stewart 1980). White neighborhood residents may have had other opportunities if it was not for the place where they lived because of their physiological characteristics, but there is no data to support that assumption. While a number of businesses operated in the neighborhood, it was bypassed by much of the commercial growth that took place in the downtown area and elsewhere in the city. Blacks in Boise remained stigmatized because of their neighborhood and white residents bore the stigma of living in "the black neighborhood." After the 1960s, the stigma of River Street as a crime-ridden ghetto became more real as upwardly mobile African Americans moved away and certain areas of the neighborhood became known for drug trafficking and prostitution (Demo 2006).

Conclusion

The stigmatization of African Americans in River Street was essential to the creation and maintenance of white privilege. Non-white groups are necessary in order to provide a contrast for whiteness. As a race, white people only exist in opposition to non-whites and, through the educated class and political system, white elites play a pivotal role in deciding non-whiteness. Over time, white privilege has become normalized in American society and whiteness has become a baseline against which other races and ethnicities are compared. This normalization has reached a point where many white people are unaware or unable to acknowledge the existence of white privilege in the United States because many of the characteristics of what it means to be white—self-sufficiency, hard-working, financial success—have become synonymous with what it means to be an American (Hartmann et al. 2009).

The future aim of the River Street Digital History Project is to talk with former residents in order to provide a more nuanced interpretation of past racial dynamics in Boise. It is hoped that the resulting interpretations will contribute valuable context for the planned archaeological interpretations and excavations.

River Street faces a new threat today. With home prices on the upswing, the City of Boise has resumed its plan to replace the neighborhood with new housing, civic buildings, and businesses that cater to the need of young, urban professionals. These new emigrants to Boise are overwhelmingly Euroamericans seeking to raise families in a safe, urbane environment. They are usually unaware of the role River Street played in the history of Boise, Idaho. Levy, Comey, and Padilla (2007:238) remark on the effects that gentrification is currently having on formerly low-income and ethnic neighborhoods like River Street. The authors explain that: "Decreases in affordable housing units have accompanied the higher prices in many places, and there are numerous reports of resident displacement from neighborhoods long ignored that now attract higher-income households." As more of the River Street Neighborhood is lost, the long movement toward eradicating Boise's black neighborhood is almost complete. The River Street Digital History Project is one way of reclaiming the past and tucking it safely out of reach of the wrecking ball.

Figure 74. Refurbished house on S. 14th Street, 2014 (White).

River Street as a Historical Memoryscape

What the heck is a memoryscape? It is a term used in geography, but it refers to a phenomenon that we all are familiar with. Human beings exist on a living planet. Earth would exist with or without us. However, we are unable to know the natural world in which we live without viewing it through the lens of our experiences and our culture. We relate to the world around us—our houses, streets, offices, hiking paths, and the rest of the world—based on the activities we have done, things we have heard, and the social rules that guide our conduct (these rules of conduct are also part of our culture). Landscapes are human constructs that come from our memories and culture. Sure, the Earth and the rest of the galaxy exists without us, but we cannot know this world without viewing it from the perspective of our culture because culture is embedded so deeply within our minds.

Landscapes are the human way of knowing the terrain upon which we live.

Landscapes exist not only in the present. They are also part of our memories. Think about it. Do you remember every single thing you encountered on your way to work/school this morning? What the names of all the streets you passed on your way home today? How did you know which way to go to get to work? You knew how to get to work and back because you know how your landscape works. If you drove, you know the rules of the road, the fastest route between your home and office, and how to get around traffic if it starts slowing you down.

You know the landscape within which you live because it is familiar to you—it is in your memory.

And, you know how to travel through your landscape because of the memories you have doing it in the past. While you may not be able to recall the location, shape, and color of every single thing on the landscape, it is familiar to you because a version of it exists in your memories.

Memoryscapes are the way human beings remember the landscapes in which they live. It is the places you can "see" in your mind when you close your eyes. For social scientists, memoryscapes are important because they help us understand the ways people make sense of the places where they live, work, and play. We social scientists want to know what other people are thinking and why they have those thoughts. Researching memoryscapes is another way to make sense of the world of human beings.

The River Street Neighborhood as a Landscape of Memory

Most of the detached, single-family dwellings in River Street have been destroyed through various development projects. The physical structures that used to make River Street a community have been lost. Most of what remains exists in the memories of people that used to live there. In 2014, I gave a presentation on how the concept of memoryscapes relates to the River Street Neighborhood. You can see a screencast of that presentation below. Or, you can check out the Slideshare version of the same presentation:

> Visit www.riverstreethistory.com to learn about the role the River Street Neighborhood played in the creation of whiteness as a distinct racial identity in Boise.

Take a tour of the River Street Neighborhood using Google Earth

We've brought the historic neighborhood to your computer screen. Harnessing the power of Google Earth, you can take a virtual tour of the River Street Neighborhood from the comfort of your own home.

The Google Earth Tour allows you to traverse the memoryscape recalled by former residents in their oral history interviews and preserved in archival documents. It also includes a description of some of the places discussed in the oral history interviews and in historical documents. You can also see photographs of the neighborhood from the past and present, and see how the neighborhood has changed throughout time as seen through historical maps.

Figure 75. 2014 Presentation on 'memoryscape' and how it relates to the River Street Neighborhood can be viewed at www.riverstreethistory.com

How to use the River Street Virtual Tour

In order to use the this virtual tour, you will need to download Google Earth (www.google.com/earth/download/). Once you've downloaded Google Earth, you can use the tour however you like. If you'd like to see it again in the future, simply move the tour up to your "My Places" tab.

NOTE: The tour currently does not work properly on an iPhone or iPad. It is only able to work on a computer (both Mac and PC).

Download the River Street Virtual Tour

Visit www.riverstreethistory.com for downloadable Google Earth files to take a virtual tour of the River Street Neighborhood on Google Earth.

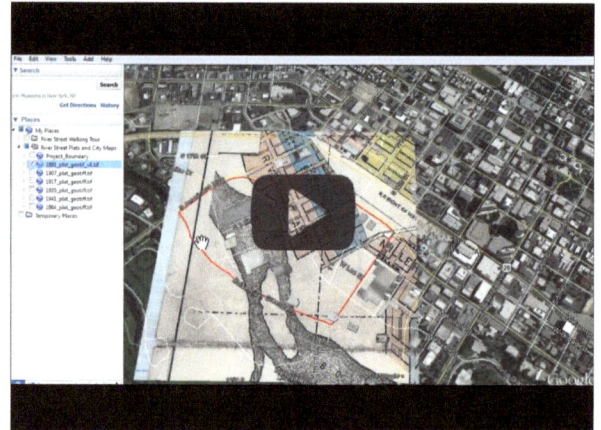

Figure 76. A brief tutorial on the Google Earth tour of the River Street Neighborhood can be found at.www.riverstreethistory.com.

The Future of the River Street Digital History Project

The River Street Neighborhood was the oldest and largest African American community in Boise, Idaho. Growing up as one of the few African Americans in Boise, I can remember learning that this neighborhood was "our place". It was where "we" used to live before the town's segregated housing codes ended and development removed most of the houses. While a few African Americans remained in the neighborhood, the vast majority of us had left by the 1970s.

I have always wondered about the role the neighborhood played in the formation and history of our community. I have also wondered how the dissolution of this neighborhood has affected Boise's African Americans since the late 1960s. There are several routes that can be taken in order to answer these questions. This River Street Digital History Project is one large step; however, historical archaeological investigations can add artifacts and archaeological data to what is known about the River Street Neighborhood.

Collecting additional oral history interviews and digitizing archival data for this website is definitely something that will continue well into the foreseeable future. Please contact me if you would like to contribute to this project by visiting www.riverstreethistory.com.

Figure 77. Sun sets over Boise, Idaho, 2014 (White).

Figure 78. University of Idaho archaeological excavations at Fort Boise, 2014 (White).

Public Archaeology Project at the Erma Hayman

In 2015, the CCDC gave the go-ahead to conduct an archaeological field school in the River Street Neighborhood. The field school will be administered by the University of Idaho and Dr. Mark Warner, chair of the Department of Sociology and Anthropology, has agreed to organize the field school for the summer of 2015. Excavations will attempt to:

- Determine the presence or absence of intact archaeological deposits in the River Street Neighborhood
- Define the location, integrity, and extent of archaeological materials on this property
- Collect information on life in the River Street Neighborhood during the late nineteenth and early twentieth century.
- Provide information that can be used to guide the CCDC's historic preservation efforts.

The field school will be six weeks long, running from 5/26/2015 through 7/3/2015. In the process of earning six college credits, students will have the opportunity to:

- Learn basic archaeological method and theory
- Participate in archaeological excavations at a historical site
- Prepare artifacts for curation
- Facilitate ethnographic interviews with the descendant community
- Work with volunteers on this groundbreaking heritage conservation project
- Hear presentations by some of Boise's most prominent historians and archaeologists

The archaeological field school will also have an accompanying public archaeology component where volunteers will have the chance to:

- Help reclaim this unwritten piece of Boise's heritage
- Participate in archaeological excavations
- Be part of the "history creation" process as you find items that haven't been seen in generations
- Learn about how archaeology works and what it can contribute to local history

56

The results of this project will be published by the end of 2015. The River Street Digital History Project website will be the information hub for all activity associated with the archaeological component.

Public interest in Boise urban archaeology has remained strong. Recent investigations by the University of Idaho at the Cyrus Jacobs-Uberuaga House and at Fort Boise have been well received by the community. Hundreds of Boiseans visited these digs. Dozens volunteered at them. The archaeological field school at the Erma Hayman House is a continuation of this strong tradition of public outreach through archaeology

River Street as an Archaeological Sensitivity Zone?

What remains of the residential neighborhood fabric of River Street has been compromised by development during the twentieth century. Few residential dwellings exist. Previous attempts to create a historical district in River Street have not been realized (for more information see Susan M. Stacy's 1995 report "River Street Reconnaissance Survey"; a document on file at the Idaho State Historic Preservation Office.) While cultural resources surveys have documented the fragmentary nature of the River Street Neighborhood as a historical resource based on its value as a part of the built environment, archaeological remnants of the neighborhood are likely to exist. The City of Boise and CCDC could create a regulatory framework that prioritizes the recovery and analysis of archaeological remains within the historical boundaries of the River Street Neighborhood. Preservation strategies like this exist in several other cities across the United States (for example, the City of Tucson has established zoning overlays that force archaeological monitoring or evaluation within eleven areas across the city).

Establishing an archaeological sensitivity zone within the historical River Street Neighborhood would be a step towards preserving and reclaiming the heritage of this rapidly vanishing place.

Conclusions

Idaho's heritage has been built upon the contributions of individuals from diverse racial and ethnic backgrounds. Despite the fact that Euro-Americans have historically comprised the majority of the state's population, important groups of African Americans, Asian immigrants, Basque, and European immigrants have played an essential role in the social development of urban centers across the state. The River Street Neighborhood was the historical home for most of the non-white population of Boise. Between the 1890s and 1960s, African-American, Basque, and European immigrants made their homes in River Street and lived amicably alongside other working-class Euro-Americans. This was one of the most diverse neighborhoods in Boise, yet its history is only now being told.

Recent advances in online technology have made the dissemination of historical information and oral histories easier than ever before. The internet also allows information to reach audiences around the world. The River Street Digital History Project uses a website to distribute oral histories and historical data to local students, teachers, historians, and communities near and far. It includes oral histories, photographs, and documents on file at repositories throughout Boise in a readily accessible manner that brings these resources to anyone with a computer and internet access. The website also includes an interpretive guided tour highlighting the neighborhood's history that can be used by anyone interested in the history of this multi-ethnic community or the rest of Boise, Idaho. The entire project preserves the memories of former residents in an easily accessible format and will increase awareness of this multi-ethnic community's unique history. It is also a means of highlighting Boise's diversity to the rest of the world.

Visit the River Street Digital History Project website at www.riverstreethistory.com

References

Beebe, Paul
1987   Developer says work to start on new offices. Idaho Statesman 6/3/1987. Statesman_6_3_1987_work_Started_on_Offices

Bird, Annie Laurie
1934   Boise: The Peace Valley. Caxton Printers, Caldwell, Idaho.

Buckner, Dorothy
1981   Interview by Mateo Osa, 23 January. Manuscript and audio tape, Lee Street Historic District Project: OH#562, Reel #375. Idaho Oral History Center, Idaho State Historical Society, Boise.

Cameron, Mindy
1971   "Renewal Asked on River Street at Boise Parlay." Idaho Daily Statesman 10/8/1971:C6–7. Daily_Statesman_10-8-1971_Renewal_Asked_on_River_Street
1970   "River Street Center: A Successful Experiment." Idaho Statesman 12/13/1970:2E. Statesman_12-13-1970_River_Street_Center

Cashin, Sheryll
2008   Race, Class, Real Estate. *Race, Poverty, and the Environment* 15(2):56–58.

Curfman, Eryn
2002   "Wall woes may force church to move." Idaho Statesman, 1/12/2002. Statesman_2002_Church_May_Move

Demo, Pam
2006   Boise's River Street Neighborhood: Lee, Ash, and Lover's Lane/Pioneer Streets, the South Side of the Tracks. Ms., Department of Anthropology, University of Idaho, Moscow.
2013   Personal communication, Boise.

Epperson, Terrence W.
2001   'A Separate House for The Christian Slaves, One for the Negro Slaves': The Archaeology of Race and Identity in Late Seventeenth-Century Virginia. *Race and the Archaeology of Identity*, Charles E. Orser, Jr., editor. University of Utah Press, Salt Lake City.

Etlinger, Charles
1987   "Black Roots Go Deep in Idaho." Idaho Statesman 2/16/1987:1. Statesman_2-16-1987_Black_Roots_Go_Deep_in_Idaho

Ewing, Carrie
1970   "Owner Donates River Street Lot; Volunteers Map Playground Plan." Idaho Statesman 8/17/1970:10. Statesman_8-17-1981_Owner_Donates_River_Street_Lot

Frankenberg, Ruth (editor)
1997   *Displacing Whiteness*. Duke University Press, Durham.

Friend, Janin
1986   Office Complex Planned Along the River. Idaho Statesman 3/29/1986. Statesman_3_29_1986_OfficeComplex_Planned_on_river

Fullilove, Mindy Thompson
2009   *Root Shock: How Tearing Up City Neighborhoods Hurts America and What We Can Do About It*. One World/Ballantine, New York.

Grote, Tom
1981   "River Street Poses Dilemma." Idaho Statesman 7/13/1981:1A. Statesman_7-13-1981_River_Street_Poses_Dilemma

Hartigan, Jr., John
1997   Establishing the Fact of Whiteness. *American Anthropologist* 99(3):495–505.
2005   *Odd Tribes: Toward a Cultural Analysis of White People*. Duke University Press, Durham, North Carolina.

Hartmann, Douglas, Joseph Gerteis, and Paul R. Croll

2009   An Empirical Assessment of Whiteness Theory: Hidden from how Many? *Social Problems* 56(3):403–424.

Hayman, Erma

1980   Interview by Mateo Osa, 17 December. Manuscript and audio tape, Lee Street Historic District Project: OH#563. Idaho Oral History Center, Idaho State Historical Society, Boise.

Heaton, John W.

2005   The Shoshone-Bannocks: Culture and Commerce at Fort Hall, 1870–1940. University of Kansas Press, Lawrenceville, Kansas.

Hyra, Derek S.

2008   *The New Urban Renewal: The Economic Transformation of Harlem and Bronzeville.* University of Chicago Press, Chicago.

Idaho Statesman

1981   "Once-thriving neighborhood exists in history alone." 3/25/1981. Statesman_3-25-1981_Once_Thriving_Neighborhood_Lives_in_Oral_History

1981   "River Street, Historic Preservation." 7/21/1981. Statesman_4_21_1981_River_Street_Historic_Preservation

Jacobson, Matthew Frye

1998   *Whiteness of a Different Color: European Immigrants and the Alchemy of Race.* Harvard University Press, Cambridge.

Levy, Diane K., Jennifer Comey, and Sandra Padilla

2007   In the Face of Gentrification: Case Studies of Local Efforts to Mitigate Displacement. *Journal of Affordable Housing and Community Development Law* 16(3):238–315.

Madsen, Brigham D.

1980   The Northern Shoshone. Caxton Printers, Caldwell.

Mercier, Laurie and Carole Simon-Smolinsk

1990   Idaho's Ethnic Heritage: Historical Overview, Vol. 1. Ethnic Heritage Project, Boise, Idaho. Document on file at the Idaho State Archives, Boise, Idaho.

Mullins, Paul

1999   *Race and Affluence: An Archaeology of African America and Consumer Culture.* Plenum Publishers, New York.

Odoshi, Denise

2005   "Boise's Lee Street area now mostly a memory." Idaho Statesman 1/26/2005:1. Statesman_1-26-2005_Lee_Street_Mostly_a_Memory

Oliver, Mamie O.

1990   Ebony: The African American Presence in Idaho State History. Document on file at the Idaho State Archives, Boise, Idaho.

Orser, Jr., Charles E.

2007   *The Archaeology of Race and Racialization in Historic America.* University Press of Florida, Gainesville.

2004   *Race and Practice in Archaeological Interpretation.* University of Pennsylvania Press, Philadelphia.

Osa, Mateo

1981   Summary of Lee Street Neighborhood. Report 93. Document on file at the Idaho State Historic Preservation Office, Boise.

Pewitt, Jana

1990   Forest River IX will join complex by the Greenbelt. Idaho Statesman 7/25/1990. Statesman_7_25_1990_Forest_River_Complex

Reichl, Alexander J.

1997   Historic Preservation and Progrowth Politics in U.S. Cities. *Urban Affairs Review* 32(4):513–535.

Roediger, David R.

2005   *Working Toward Whiteness: How*

America's Immigrants became White. Basic Books, Cambridge, Massachusetts.

1991 *The Wages of Whiteness: Race and the Making of the American Working Class.* Verso, London, United Kingdom.

Savage, W. Sherman
1928 "The Negro in the History of the Pacific Northwest." The Journal of Negro History, 13(3):255–264.

Stacy, Susan M.
1995 River Street Area Reconnaissance Survey. Idaho Historic Properties Survey Report #222. Prepared for the Boise City Historic Preservation Commission, Boise, Idaho. Document on file at the Idaho State Historic Preservation Office, Boise, Idaho.

Stewart, Bessie
1980 Interview by Mateo Osa, 17 January. Manuscript and audio tape, Lee Street Historic District Project: OH#565, Idaho Oral History Center, Idaho State Historical Society, Boise.

Stringfellow, Rosalie
1950 "Keys to St. Paul's Church Parsonage Presented to Pastor." Idaho Daily Statesman, 3/28/1850. Statesman_1950_St_Pauls_Parsonage

Waite, Thornton
n.d. "Boise: On the Main Line at Last." The Streamliner. Union Pacific Historical Society, Cheyanne, Wyoming.

Wacquant, Loïs
2010 Urban Desolation and Symbolic Denigration in the Hyperghetto. *Social Psychology Quarterly* 73(3):215–219.

Walker, Jr., Deward E.
1978 Indians of Idaho. Anthropological Monographs of the University of Idaho, Moscow, Idaho.

Whaley, Susan
2002 "Faith of a Congregation." Idaho Statesman, 2/3/2002:1,7. Statesman_2002_Faith_of_congregation1

White, III, William A.
2014 Memoryscapes, Whiteness, and River Street: How African Americans Helped Maintain Euroamerican Identity in Boise, Idaho. Unpublished presentation given at the Society for Historical Archaeology Annual Conference, Quebec City, Canada.

Winn, Christian A.
2001 Down by the River: The Past, Present, and Future of a Historic Boise Neighborhood. Boise Weekly, Nov. 28–Dec.4. Boise_Weekly_11-28--12-4-2001_Down_by_the_River

Wolf, Eric
1997 Introduction, Europe and the People without History. University of California Press, 3¬23.

Wyatt, Liz
2000 "River Street Neighborhood shows signs of renaissance." Idaho Statesman 6/11/2000: 1A,6A–7A. Statesman_6-11-2000_River_Street_Revival

Wynn, Pat
1973 "The Role of St. Paul's Church as Cultural, Spiritual Center." Idaho Statesman 1/28/1973:4E. Statesman_1973_St_paul_cultural_Center

Zarkin, David
1968 "Once-Proud River Street Area Hosted Boise's Cultural, Sporting Activities." Idaho Daily Statesman, 3/11/1968:14. Statesman_3-11-1968_River_Street_Hosted_Cultural_Activities

1968 "Variety of Zoning in Vicinity of Boise River Street Complicates Maintaining Standards in Residences." Idaho Daily Statesman, 3-12-68:pg. 5–C1. Daily_Statesman_3-12-1968_Zoning_in_River_Street_Complicates_Maintaining_Standards

www.ingramcontent.com/pod-product-compliance
Lightning Source LLC
Chambersburg PA
CBHW041425090426
42741CB00002B/35